# ARE YOU

# SMART ENOUGH

★★★★★ TO BE A ★★★★★

# SECRET
# AGENT?

**Portable Press**
An imprint of Printers Row Publishing Group
10350 Barnes Canyon Road, Suite 100, San Diego, CA 92121
www.portablepress.com • mail@portablepress.com

Printers Row Publishing Group is a division of Readerlink Distribution Services, LLC.
Portable Press is a registered trademark of Readerlink Distribution Services, LLC.

All notations of errors or omissions should be addressed to Portable Press, Editorial Department, at the above address. All other correspondence (author inquiries, permissions) concerning the content of this book should be addressed to The Bright Press, part of The Quarto Group, Level 1, Ovest House, 58 West Street, Brighton, UK, BN1 2RA.

Publisher: Peter Norton
Associate Publisher: Ana Parker
Publishing/Editorial Team: Kathryn C. Dalby, Lauren Taniguchi
Editorial Team: JoAnn Padgett, Melinda Allman, Dan Mansfield

Conceived and designed by The Bright Press, part of The Quarto Group,
Level 1, Ovest House, 58 West Street, Brighton, UK, BN1 2RA
Publisher: Mark Searle
Creative director: James Evans
Managing editor: Jacqui Sayers
In-house editor: Judith Chamberlain
Cover and interior design: Matt Windsor
Text: John Gillard

ISBN: 978-1-64517-048-8

23 22 21 20 19   1 2 3 4 5

Printed in Singapore

# ARE YOU
# SMART ENOUGH
★★★★★ TO BE A ★★★★★
# SECRET
# AGENT?

## THE UNOFFICIAL CIA
## PUZZLE BOOK

**PORTABLE PRESS**

SAN DIEGO, CALIFORNIA

# CONTENTS

# INTRODUCTION

To be successful in the world of espionage takes a hugely varied skill set. You must be confident and smart, and able to adjust to your surroundings and evade suspicion, while maintaining observation and awareness at all times. You will find yourself in unusual locations, under time pressures, and in mentally and physically demanding situations. Governments rely on their secret agents to collect key intelligence on threats to the nation. These can come from terrorist groups, hackers of financial and military systems, foreign operatives intent on gathering their own intelligence, and enemies of the state closer to home.

Operations can be in the field, often on the streets of the world's capitals, and sometimes behind enemy lines in highly volatile locations. They can be based at headquarters—analyzing data, documents, transcripts of conversations, and surveillance images, and scoping potential threats. All operations require high levels of logical and lateral thinking, memory and perception, espionage techniques, and a good working knowledge of international relations and the lessons of the recent past.

All of these essential skills are tested in this book, from cracking a safe to deciphering code, and from disarming a gunman to locating global conflict zones. Above all, your country needs talented individuals to maintain national security. The question is this: Are you smart enough to be a secret agent?

# LOGIC AND LATERAL THINKING

# CRACK THE SAFE

Can you crack the safe's code and extract the documents within?

With the exception of three numbers, every number in the outer ring of the safe dial is linked in some way. Can you work out in what way they are linked and which three numbers are the odd ones out? Insert the three correct numbers in the combination lock to crack the safe.

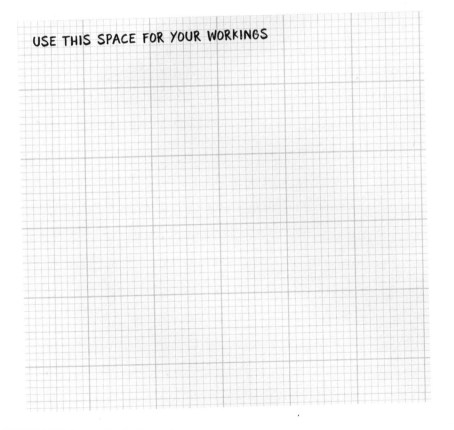

USE THIS SPACE FOR YOUR WORKINGS

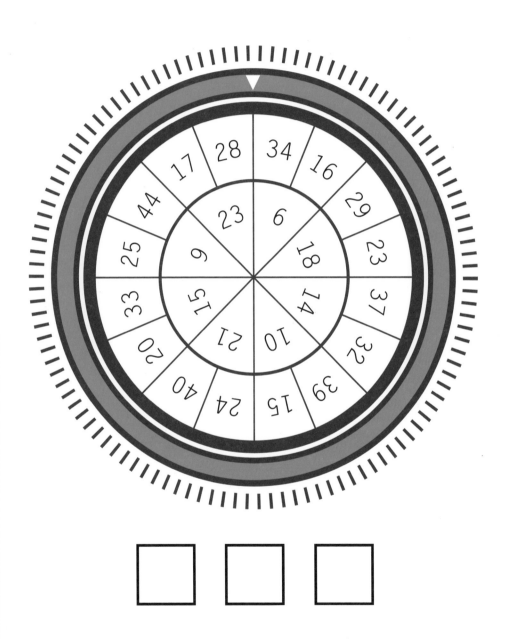

# NEXT ASSIGNMENT

You have been handed your next assignment. The start date of a covert operation you are to be involved in has been encrypted. You have been provided with five rows of symbols and a series of historical events. You are told the first row of symbols represents the year World War II ended. Can you use this information to unlock the final line of code and work out the start date of the covert mission?

```
The end of the U.S. Civil War
The end of World War II
The Berlin Wall comes down
September 11 attack on the United States
```

USE THIS SPACE FOR YOUR WORKINGS

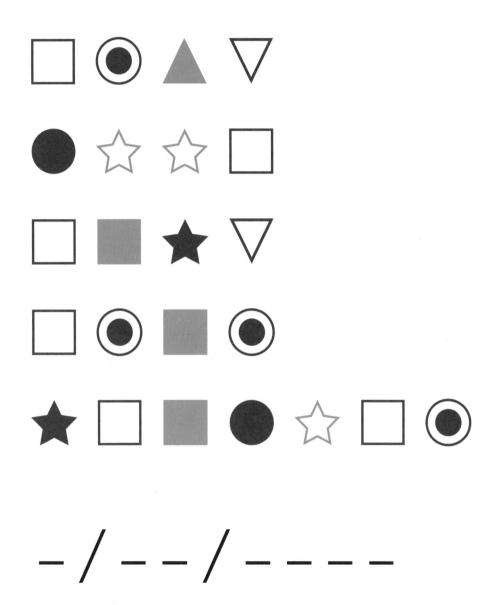

# WHAT DID SHE DO?

In 1960 the British MI6 operative Daphne Park, who was posted in the African nation of the Congo, was confronted with a life-threatening situation that required quick thinking and ingenuity. While driving her Citroën 2CV she saw a machete-wielding mob with a hatred for colonial powers heading toward her. What did she do?

☐ A. She stopped, pulled out her diplomatic papers, and waved them out of the window.
☐ B. She put a journalist ID and camera around her neck.
☐ C. She pulled out a gun, firing two shots into the air from the car window.
☐ D. She stopped the car, opened the hood, and said, "Thank goodness you've come along—I think I have a problem with my carburetor."

# HIDDEN IN NUMBERS

You are working with five agents in the field. Each agent has been assigned a number that links to their names.

```
JAN is agent 10
JANE is agent 12
SEAN is agent 16
JON is agent 15
JOHANNES is agent ?
```

What number has been assigned to Johannes?

---

You have received the message below from Agent 12. She has not given you a key to decipher the code, so you believe there to be another way in which to read the lines of numbers. Can you work out what the method might be? And can you spell out the messages hidden in the numbers?

```
5335   7718
771  51  337
53045  57735  345
```

# SWITCHED DRINKS?

You are in a hotel bar having drinks with two new business associates. You suspect your drink was switched when you reached down to retrieve papers from your briefcase. You are sure your glass was a little less than half full previously and suspect it is now more than half full. There are no markings on the glass. How can you tell for sure if the glass is now more than half full?

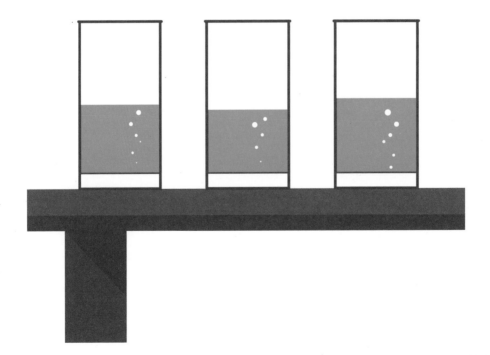

# STEPS TO FREEDOM

There are 87 steps from the reflecting pool to the Abraham Lincoln memorial chamber in Washington, D.C. Starting at step 0, can you make your way through the numbered boxes below to find a path to step 87 and reach the memorial? The total number of the steps you take along the way must add up to 87. You can make as many moves as you like, both upward and downward, but you must not retrace any of your steps.

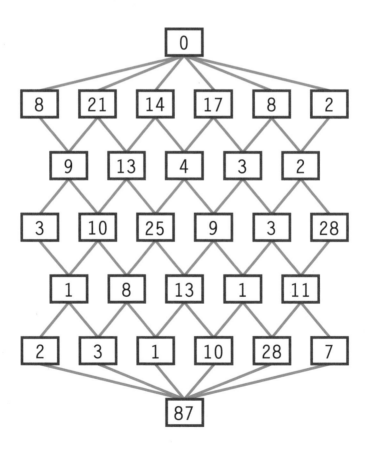

# TWO TRAINS

Intelligence suggests a meeting is due to take place between a suspected double agent and a member of an enemy organization. The targets are traveling by train from separate locations. The starting point of both targets is known, but the time and place of the meeting is not. You also know the trains on which the targets are traveling are 600km (373 miles) apart and both are departing at 2:00 p.m. The suspected double agent is traveling from the west on a train moving at an average speed of 50km/h (31 miles per hour). The member of the enemy organization is traveling from the east on a train moving at 70km/h (44 miles per hour). There are 23 stations along the route, approximately 25km (16 miles) apart. Can you work out at which station the meeting will take place and at what time?

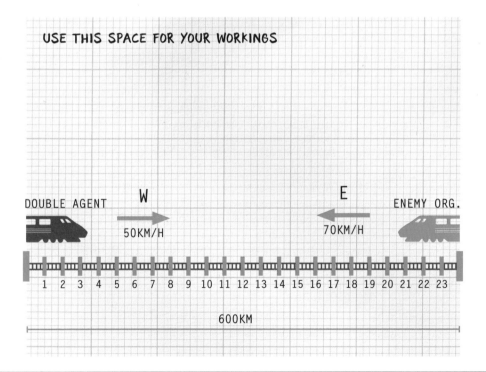

USE THIS SPACE FOR YOUR WORKINGS

DOUBLE AGENT   W                    E           ENEMY ORG.

50KM/H                    70KM/H

1  2  3  4  5  6  7  8  9  10  11  12  13  14  15  16  17  18  19  20  21  22  23

600KM

# THE SAFEST ROUTE

You must meet a highly valuable informer who has details of an alleged terrorist cell working within the capital city. You have arranged to meet the informer on the banks of a river which runs through a small farming village. You must disclose the exact location to them. You suspect you are under observation and must meet the informer and return to a safe house as quickly as possible. You will be leaving from the village church and walking across open fields. It is imperative you find the quickest route from the church, to the riverbank, and then to the safe house. There is an exact point on the riverbank that will ensure the shortest possible journey. Using the map of the area below, mark the exact spot you have chosen to meet.

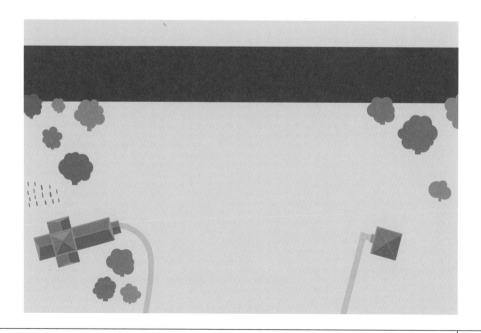

# NINE DOTS

Using four continuous straight lines, and without raising your pen from the page or retracing the path of your lines, can you join all nine of the dots?

# RETRIEVING THE DOCUMENTS

You must enter an office building and retrieve documents from the workstation marked X on the schematic below. Your technical operations team has augmented a CCTV time-lapse, allowing you a very short time collecting data from each workstation while evading security. You must enter every workstation before reaching the documents. Your starting point is a small entrance point in which you have time to leave and return to if required. Can you plot a route that leads to the documents while entering every workstation only once?

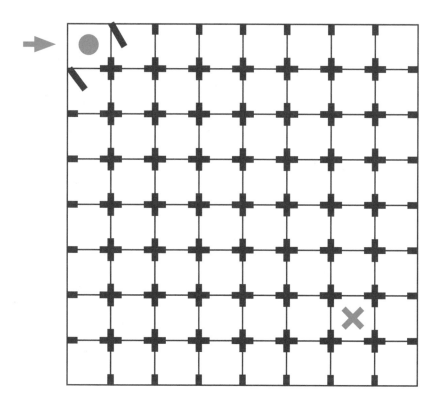

# MENTAL AGILITY

Mental agility and speed of thought are key skills in a secret agent's repertoire. Test your skills with this series of short yet challenging mental agility exercises. Set yourself a target of 15, 30, or 45 minutes to crack the codes, work out the conundrums, and test your logic and lateral thinking under time pressure.

1. Decipher the encrypted message from the codetext below. The key is:
A = 14, N = 1

```
7 21 18     17 2 8 15 25 18
14 20 18 1 7     21 14 6
18 6 16 14 3 18 17     7 2
14 25 20 22 18 5 6
10 22 7 21     19 22 25 18
```

2. How many squares are there on a chessboard?

3. Why do you have to climb higher to reach the top of the Eiffel Tower in Paris in the summer than in the winter?

_____

4. Can you work out this coded meeting time outside the hospital?
"Meet Dr. Awkward at his favorite time of the day"

_____

5. What takes up 2% of its home yet uses 20% of its home's energy?

_____

6. If:
1 x 2 = 3
3 x 4 = 21
5 x 6 = 55
7 x 8 = 105
Then:
6 x 5 = ?

_____

7. In which years did the following events take place? Clue: Each year is unique in the same way.

• The first banknotes in Europe are issued by Sweden

_____

• Thomas Cook returns to the Western world from his around-the-world voyage, during which he discovered Australia

_____

• U.S. president James A. Garfield is assassinated

_____

• The USSR is dissolved, bringing about the end of the Cold War

_____

8. If:

2 = 6

3 = 12

4 = 20

5 = 30

6 = 42

10 = ?

9. You are invited to attend your team leader's 20th wedding anniversary. In fact, it is a code for the location of your next covert mission. Where are you going?

10. The sixteen words below can be grouped into four distinct sets of four based on common links between the words in each grouping. Be careful: some of the words can be linked to words that are not part of a group of four.

| Peace | Pocket | Foil | Bird |
| Cue | Wailing | Jack | Pot |
| Berlin | Sabbath | Stripes | Nails |
| Rack | Ball | Great | Golf club |

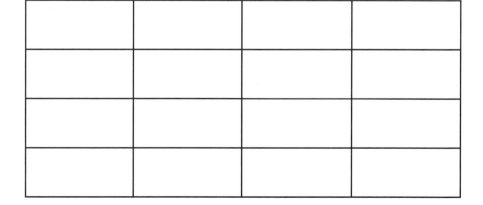

# DRINKING LIMITS

Two CIA agents are having a beer in a bar. One of the agents has set herself a self-discipline guideline for the month of February that she will only drink 400ml, or a little under one pint, of beer per day. The agent's colleague accepts that this is a noble test and a surefire health benefit. They order two beers and ask the bartender that one glass of beer be only 400ml in quantity. The bartender explains the problem they have: he has only a 700ml glass or a 500ml glass. Being a stickler for the rules she has set herself, the agent insists she and her colleague find a way to measure out exactly 400ml using the 700ml and 500ml glasses—this despite there being no markings on either glass, nor any measuring equipment. They set about trying to crack the problem. They are also not averse to pouring away beer and buying any refills, if needed. By the time they leave the bar, the agent is happy in the knowledge that she has consumed 400ml of beer. How did she do it? On a side note, the agent managed to find the most efficient method possible. Can you do the same?

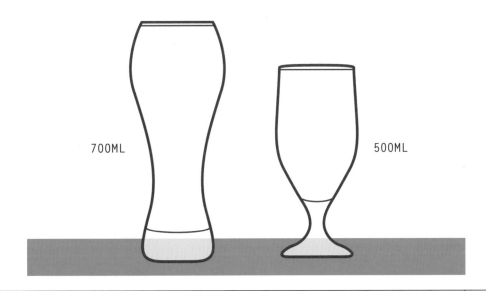

700ML  500ML

# THE FINAL MEETING

Intelligence sources have uncovered a potential security threat. A series of business meetings have been planned between a suspected spy and five business people from key industries, including a business contracted to supply arms to the military. The timings for the first five meeting times have been uncovered, but it is the final meeting, the time of which is unknown, that is considered the greatest risk to national security. The known meetings are all early in the morning and due to take place in a small coffee shop uptown. The counter-espionage team has uncovered four potential meeting times for the final day. Can you see a pattern in the days and times of the previous meetings that might suggest a concrete time for the final meeting?

| Known meeting times | | Possible Saturday meeting times |
|---|---|---|
| Monday | 6:30 | 6:15 |
| Tuesday | 7:30 | 7:45 |
| Wednesday | 9:35 | 8:30 |
| Thursday | 8:45 | 9:35 |
| Friday | 6:40 | |

# THE MILLIONAIRE

You suspect an eccentric entrepreneur is a spy. You have arranged to meet him in a restaurant for dinner. You are looking for clues as to whether your suspicions may be correct. During the course of the conversation the businessman explains how he saved his first million. You attempt to solve the puzzle, but believe him simply to be an eccentric millionaire.

One day he saved 1 cent, the next day he saved 2 cents, the next day he saved 4 cents. He continued to save money in this way, doubling the previous day's saving. He poses the question: How many days did it take him to save $1 million?

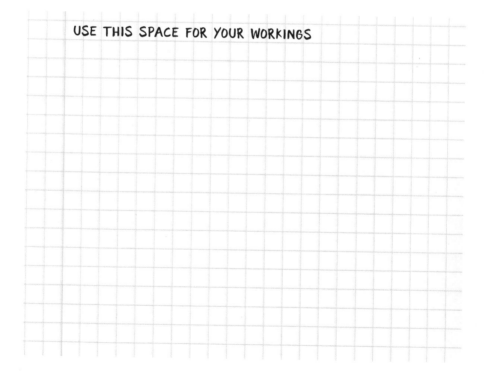

USE THIS SPACE FOR YOUR WORKINGS

# MATCHSTICKS

You are holed up in a safe house with another agent. You are in a country that has been overtaken by an anti-Western military junta. The safe house is very basic: you have a table, two chairs, two beds, some basic food supplies, and a box of matches. You are awaiting instructions on how to exit the country safely, but it could take hours, if not days, to come. Your colleague suggests you must maintain mental focus and reduce the stress of your situation. He takes the box of matches and poses a series of puzzles. Can you maintain focus and manage stress levels in order to solve the ten matchstick puzzles?

1. Move three matchsticks to make four squares

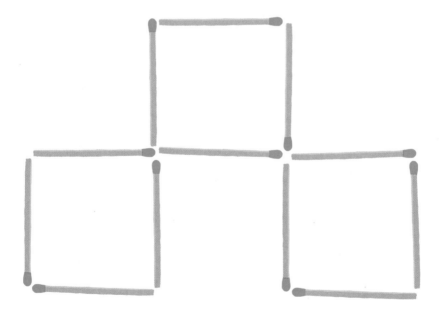

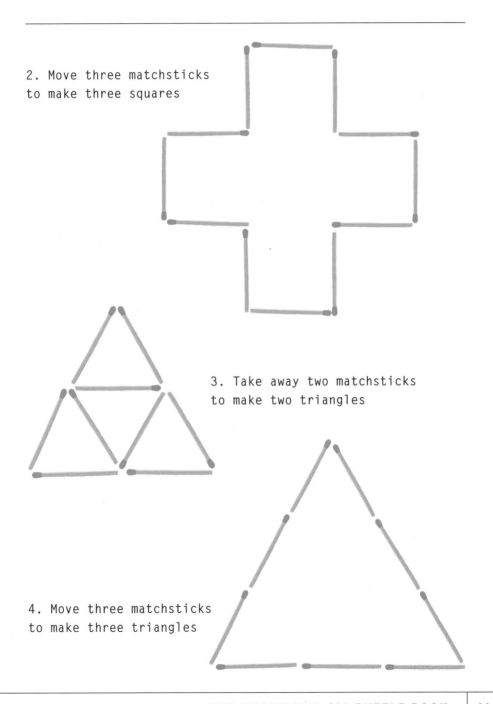

2. Move three matchsticks
to make three squares

3. Take away two matchsticks
to make two triangles

4. Move three matchsticks
to make three triangles

5. Move two matchsticks to make three triangles

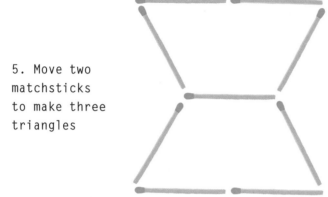

6. Move two matchsticks to make this a correct calculation

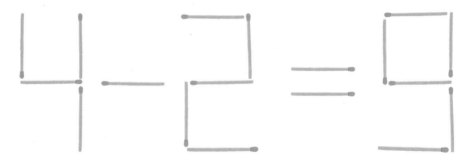

7. Add two matchsticks to make this a correct calculation

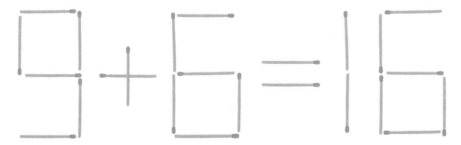

8. Move two matchsticks to make the highest number possible (without using any mathematical symbols)

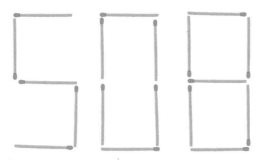

9. Move one matchstick to make this a correct calculation

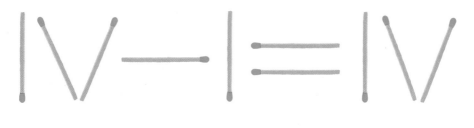

10. Halve twelve to make seven (you can add matchsticks, discard them, rearrange them, do whatever you have to do)

# A TIMELY MEETING

You are due to attend a meeting with your team leader, who is a stickler for punctuality (to the very second!). You are sitting at your desk, looking at the analog clock on the wall and scratching your head. It is 12:00 p.m. Your team leader has just explained that the meeting will take place when the hour hand and the minute hand are next in exactly the same position, as they are now, at noon. What time, to the second, is the meeting?

USE THIS SPACE FOR YOUR WORKINGS

# A CRIME SCENE

Below is a crime scene in a public restroom: a double agent who has been providing crucial intelligence for some time has been found dead, slumped next to the middle of three urinals. There is blood on and below the urinal. No witnesses have come forward, although you have reason to believe two men were at the scene. What single clue (which has already been mentioned) is there that might suggest two men were at the scene, either immediately prior to or during the suspected murder? Can you provide an explanation as to how this clue can be used to place two men at the scene of the crime?

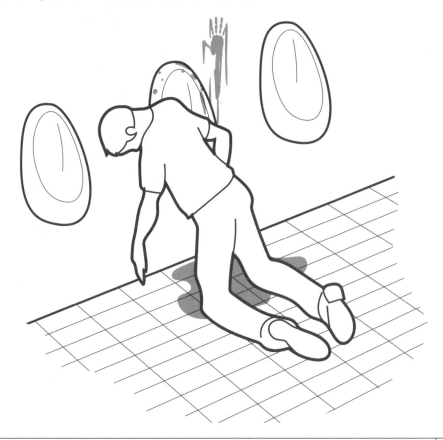

# THE SHOPPING LIST

You must pick up an important dossier from someone who will be waiting in the hallway of a hotel. You know you must enter the elevator and travel up several stories, but the exact level is as yet unknown. You have been given the following message, encrypted as a shopping list, and know you must add a total of ten digits together to get the answer. Which floor should you go to?

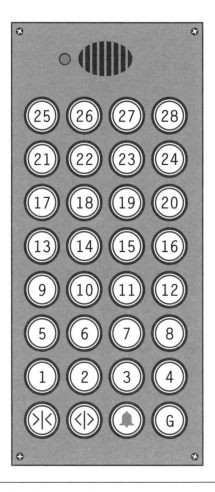

A pie
(one that is round)

Two dates:

A Christmas present

Twelve red roses

# FOUR HATS

Four field agents have been captured in hostile territory. The group that has captured them are more intent on playing games than using their prisoners as bargaining chips for financial or political gain. All four detainees are made to put on a hat. They are told that two of them have been made to wear black hats and two white, though they do not know the color of their own hat. One is placed facing a wall. The other three are lined up on the other side of the wall, one behind the other. They cannot see anything other than what is directly in front of them.

All four detainees are told they will be shot unless one of them is able to speak out within twenty seconds and confirm the color of the hat they are wearing. The confirmation must be accompanied by a logical explanation as to how they can be certain of the correct answer. A correct answer without this accompanying explanation will result in all four being shot immediately. Which one of them speaks out, declaring the color of their hat? And how can they be so certain?

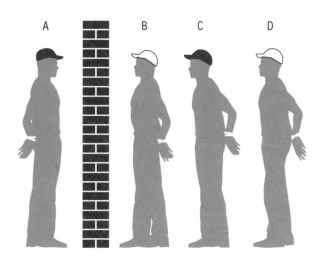

# ELEVEN GRENADES

Three field agents are sent on a dangerous mission in a highly volatile region. They are to be equipped with a full selection of firepower. Of the twelve grenades allocated to them, they are instructed to distribute them as follows:

Agent 1 is to be supplied with half
Agent 2 is to be supplied with a quarter
Agent 3 is to be supplied with a sixth

A final audit has shown one of the grenades to be defective, leaving only eleven effective grenades. How can the eleven grenades be divided between the three agents while instructions are maintained? The integrity of the devices must not be affected in any way.

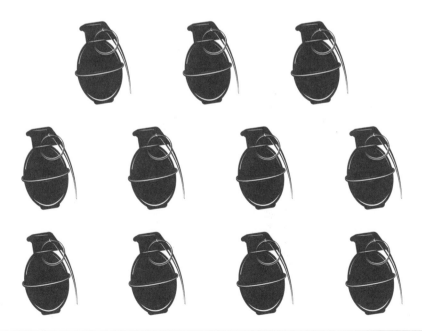

# HOW MANY HANDSHAKES?

You are working undercover, posing as a business person. You are eating out at a restaurant with three business associates. When you all arrived you shook hands with one another. There is a silence following the initial pleasantries and small talk. You take the opportunity to gauge the mental agility of the associates, as well as gently breaking the ice, by posing a question. You ask the three of them, "When we all met here tonight, how many handshakes were there?" The question has the desired effect. There is some careful pondering and some lighthearted disagreement between all three of them. One of them gives the answer that there were four handshakes; one of them says there were six; and the third offers twelve. One of the answers is correct. Which one: four, six, or twelve?

# THE BRIEFCASE

You have come into possession of a briefcase, which you are told contains vital information regarding money-laundering activities by a terrorist organization. The briefcase is locked with a security code, and it cannot be opened with force, as it is likely to contain a content-destruction security function. A codetext has been found, but there is no encryption key. It is believed this codetext hides the combination that will unlock the briefcase. Using numbers 1 to 9, you must find this four-digit combination. There are seven possible solutions to the challenge of forming a meaningful and correct calculation from the codetext, replacing the letters for numbers. Only the highest possible correct solution will release the vital documents inside. Can you find it?

TWO + TWO = FOUR

# NUMBER SQUARES

You've been handed a very strange-looking die. It has a series of seemingly random numbers across four of its sides. One of the numbers has been replaced with an asterisk *. What is the missing number?

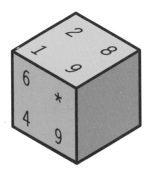

The four sides have the following numbers on them.

| 5 | 7 |
|---|---|
| 5 | 3 |

| 2 | 8 |
|---|---|
| 1 | 9 |

| 7 | 3 |
|---|---|
| 2 | 8 |

| 6 | * |
|---|---|
| 4 | 9 |

* = _____

# SIX PENCILS

You have raided the stationery cupboard at HQ and picked up six pencils you found lying on the bottom shelf. You smile because some time ago you were set a challenge by an old school friend that involved exactly six pencils. You can't remember the answer but you remember the challenge. It was this: can you make four equilateral triangles using all six pencils?

# LINKING THE PORTS

Five ships are departing from five major ports across the globe, represented by large circles. Each ship must travel to the location marked with the corresponding smaller circle. The routes taken by the ships must not cross. Can you plot the courses of these five ships so that none of their paths cross?

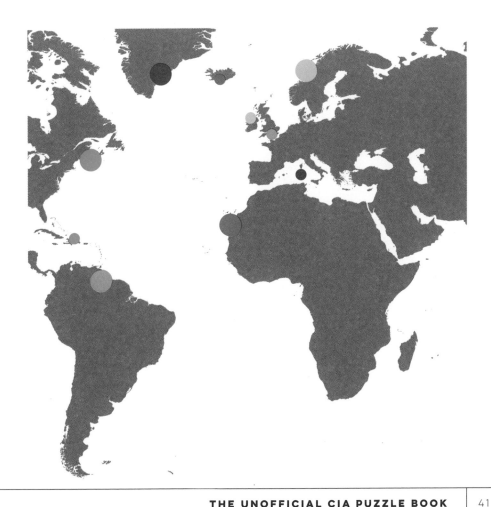

# SECRETS ON A BOOKSHELF

Two books on a shelf in a library contain hidden secrets within their pages. Can you spot which two book titles contain a particular type of word, and thus uncover their secrets?

# HIDDEN CARGO

You have been tipped off by an informer that four shipping containers will be arriving at a port depot. A number of military-grade weapons are being shipped into the country and will be delivered to a terrorist cell across varying locations. The cargo must be tracked to its final destination, but the exact time of its arrival is as yet unknown. You have received the following information: of the four containers, the first will arrive at 5:00 a.m. and the last at 9:00 p.m. The two shipments in between have staged arrival times separated by equal periods. What times will shipments 2 and 3 arrive at the port?

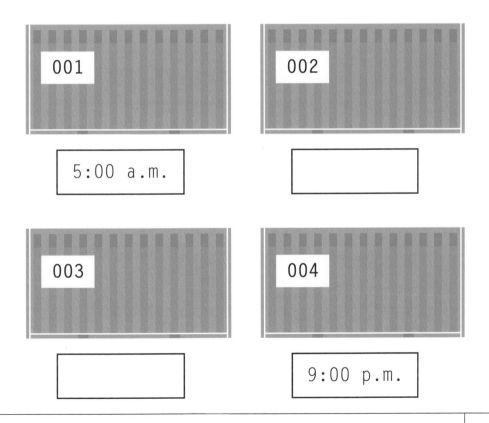

001 — 5:00 a.m.

002 —

003 —

004 — 9:00 p.m.

# CODE NAME RIDDLES

A series of project code names are hidden in riddles. Solve the riddles to reveal the code names. The answers to riddles 8 and 9 contain a further secret within them. Between these two answers are hidden the time of a clandestine meeting with a foreign operative who is willing to share vital human intelligence.

1. What goes up but can never go down?

_____

2. What can travel around the world without leaving the corner?

_____

3. A woman was born in 1963, yet today is her 21st birthday. How is this possible?

_____

4. When you say its name it is no longer there. What is it?

_____

5. What do you start when it's red and stop when it's green?

6. What do you throw away when you need it, and bring back when you're done?

7. It lives when light shines and dies when light fades. What is it?

8. What starts with an "e," ends with an "e," and contains one letter?

9. A Buddhist regrets it. When you die you can take it with you. And it is faster than the speed of light. What is it?

# INTERNATIONAL
# AFFAIRS

# GLOBAL LINKS

Can you identify the common element or theme within each of the sets below?

1. If China is Shanghai
Netherlands is Rotterdam
France is Marseille
The UAE is Dubai

Then the United States is ?

_____

2. Antigua and Barbuda
Argentina
Kiribati
Uruguay
Macedonia
?

_____

3. What links the flags
of Canada, Lebanon, and
Equatorial Guinea?

_____

4. What links the flags of
Cyprus and Kosovo?

_____

5. What links the flags of
Egypt and Albania?

_____

6. If Nigeria is Lagos
Japan is Tokyo
India is Delhi
Canada is Toronto

Then Brazil is ?

_____

7. What literally links
Russia and the United
States (once a year)?

_____

8. In what way are the countries A through E related? Choose one of the three countries labeled 1, 2, and 3 at the bottom of the page to complete the sequence.

If A.= _____                and B.= _____

and C.= _____                and D.= _____

then E.= ? _____

           1.           2.           3.

# FLAGS OF THE WORLD

As a secret agent, you must store as many reference points as possible that might allow you to place information you receive and observations you make as quickly and instinctively as possible. This ensures the maximum harvest of clues from observations and analysis. National flags are an essential reference point. Knowledge may allow you to place the origins of a vehicle, the nationality of a suspect, or give context to documents.

1. Identify the countries whose flags are shown below.

A. _____

B. _____

C. _____

D. _____

**2.1. Which country's flag is shown above?**
☐ Bahrain
☐ Tuvalu
☐ Nepal
☐ Papua New Guinea

**2.2. What is unique about this flag?**

**3.1. How many countries have a flag containing a cross (including saltires and crosses within their emblems)?**
☐ 17   ☐ 27   ☐ 37   ☐ 47

**3.2. How many of them can you name?**

**4. Of the flags shown below, which one is the flag of Algeria?**

☐ A

☐ B

☐ C

☐ D

# CONFLICT ZONE FACT FILES

Which country is being shown in each of the four fact files that follow?

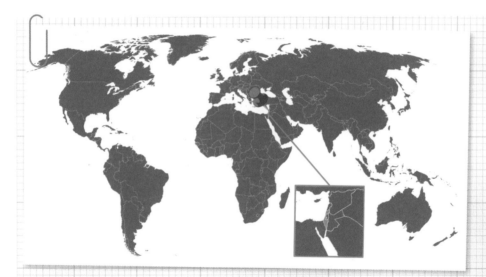

**CONFLICT ZONE STATUS\*:**

\*Council of Foreign Relations/
Global Conflict Tracker
Conflict Zone Status based on
impact on U.S. interests

**COUNTRY NAME:**

Formed: 1949
Population: 8,424,904
Area: 8,019 square miles
GDP per capita: $36,400
Imports: $68.61 billion
Exports: $58.67 billion
Religions: Jewish 74.5%,
          Muslim 17.7%
Literacy: 97.8%

1

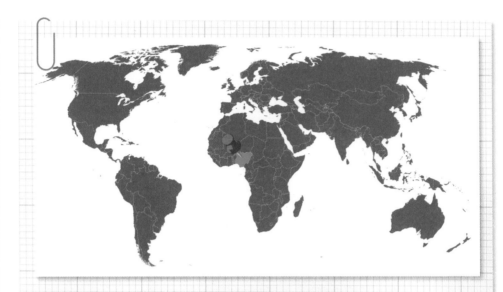

**CONFLICT ZONE STATUS*:**

*Council of Foreign Relations/ Global Conflict Tracker Conflict Zone Status based on impact on U.S. interests

**COUNTRY NAME:**

Formed: 1963
Population: 203,452,505
Area: 356,669 square miles
GDP per capita: $5,900
Imports: $35.24 billion
Exports: $40.81 billion
Religions: 51.6% Muslim,
        11.2% Roman Catholic
Literacy: 59.6%

2

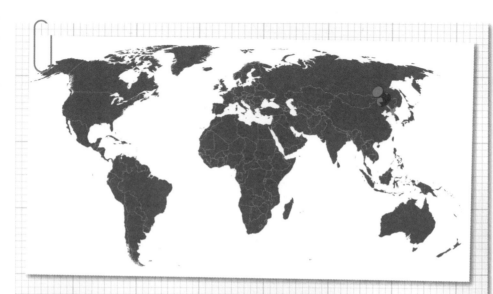

## CONFLICT ZONE STATUS*:

*Council of Foreign Relations/
Global Conflict Tracker
Conflict Zone Status based on
impact on U.S. interests

## COUNTRY NAME:

Formed: 1945
Population: 25,381,085
Area: 46,540 square miles
GDP per capita: $1,700
Imports: $43.75 billion
Exports: $45.82 billion
Religions*: 64.3% Atheist,
          16% Shamanism
Literacy: 100% (self-reported)

*2005 estimates: Religious
Intelligence UK agency

**3**

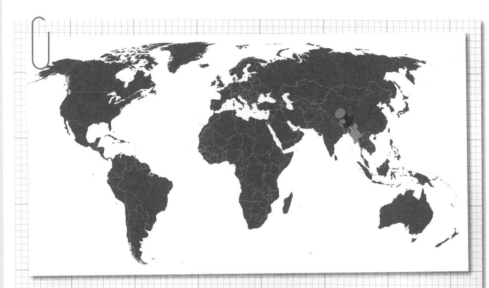

## CONFLICT ZONE STATUS*:

*Council of Foreign Relations/
Global Conflict Tracker
Conflict Zone Status based on
impact on U.S. interests

## COUNTRY NAME:

Formed: 1948
Population: 55,622,506
Area: 261,228 square miles
GDP per capita: $6,300
Imports: $15.78 billion
Exports: $9.83 billion
Religions: 87.9% Buddhist,
          6.2% Christian
Literacy: 75.6%

**4**

# WORLD INTELLIGENCE AGENCIES

It is essential to have knowledge of intelligence agencies across the globe. There is an old adage in the secret service world: "There are friendly nations, but no friendly intelligence services."* The streets of the world capitals and beyond are a battleground for intelligence agencies, and adversaries must be known.

Match the fifteen intelligence agencies opposite with their country below. Can you also highlight the "5 Eyes" nations—an intelligence-sharing security alliance between five English-speaking nations set up to combat global terrorism?

COUNTRIES:

1. Afghanistan: _____

2. Australia: _____

3. Canada: _____

4. China: _____

5. Germany: _____

6. Iran: _____

7. Israel: _____

8. Japan: _____

9. New Zealand: _____

10. North Korea: _____

11. Pakistan: _____

12. Russia: _____

13. South Africa: _____

14. United Kingdom: _____

15. United States: _____

## THE WORLD'S INTELLIGENCE AGENCIES:

A. VAJA (Ministry of Intelligence)

B. Mossad G. NDS (National Directorate of Security)

C. ASIO (<country name> Security Intelligence Organisation)

D. MSS (Ministry of State Security)

E. NICOC (National Intelligence Co-ordinating Committee)

F. CIRO (Cabinet Intelligence and Research Office)

G. NDS (National Directorate of Security)

H. CIA (Central Intelligence Agency)

I. NZSIS (<country name> Security Intelligence Service)

J. Reconnaissance General Bureau

K. CSIS (<country name> Security Intelligence Service)

L. BND (Bundesnachrichtendienst)

M. FSB (Federal Security Service)

N. ISI (Inter-Services Intelligence)

O. SIS/MI6 (Secret Intelligence Service)

* The quote is from James M. Olson, who served in the Directorate of Operations and is now on the faculty of the George Bush School of Government and Public Service at Texas A&M University.

# WHERE ARE YOU? MOUNTAIN RANGES

Can you ascertain which continent you are looking at by analyzing the images of mountain ranges below?

A. ALPS (EUROPE)    B. ANDES (SOUTH AMERICA)
C. DRAKENSBERG (AFRICA)    D. HIMALAYAS (ASIA)

1.

2.

3.

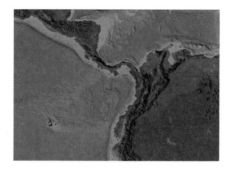

4.

# A NUMBERS GAME

Find the answers to the facts below using the numbers at the bottom of the page.

1. The population of China

_____

2. The height of Mount Everest (feet)

_____

3. Number of airports in the world

_____

4. Size of the world's largest island, Greenland (square miles)

_____

5. The height of Angel Falls (feet)

_____

6. Number of internet users in Iran

_____

7. Number of people without electricity in the world

_____

8. The GDP of Costa Rica (U.S. dollars, 2017)

_____

29,029          3212          1.4 BILLION

41,820     1.1 BILLION          83.94 BILLION

810,815          36.1 MILLION

# WHAT COMES NEXT?

By working out the connection between the four entries in each set of information below, can you complete the fifth entry?

Iran = Abadan
Montreal = Mirabel
Venice = Marco Polo
La Paz = J.F. Kennedy
Washington, D.C. = ?

1.

_____

South Africa = Volksraad
North Korea = National
 Assembly
Israel = Knesset
United States = Congress
UK = ?

2.

_____

UK = FTSE
Hong Kong = Hang Seng
United States = Dow Jones
China = SSE Composite
Japan = ?

3.

_____

Spain = ETA
Palestine = PLO
Philippines = CPLA
Sri Lanka = Tamil Tigers
Ireland = ?

4.

_____

1983 = Lech Wałesa (Poland)
1991 = Aung San Suu Kyi
 (Myanmar)
1994 = Yasser Arafat
 (Palestine), Shimon Peres
 (Israel), Yitzhak Rabin
 (Israel)
2005 = Agence
 Internationale de
 L'Energie (170 member
 states)
1993 = ?

5.

_____

_____

Bolivia = Boliviano
Gambia = Dalasi
Latvia = Lat
Qatar = Dirhams
France = ?

6.

_____

Nevada = White Sands
New Mexico = Los Alamos
Barents Sea (Russia) = Kola
  Launch Area
Kiribati (UK) = Malden
  Island
Marshall Islands = ?

7.

_____

France = The Eiffel Tower
United States = Niagara
  Falls
Greece = Acropolis of
  Athens
Peru = Machu Picchu
Brazil = ?

8.

_____

Afghanistan = Noshaq
Argentina = Aconcagua
Hungary = Kékes
UK = Ben Nevis
Turkey = ?

9.

_____

Burkina Faso = French
Kyrgyzstan = Russian
Maldives = Dhivehi
Moldova = Romanian
Mozambique = ?

10.

_____

# ABANDONED LOCATIONS

Sources have disclosed images and fragmented details of abandoned locations being used for clandestine meetings, exchanges of "dirty" money, and arms drop-offs by enemies of the state. You have been tasked with following the trail and uncovering the whereabouts of these locations. Using the recently obtained images and snippets of information provided below, can you work out the country in which each of these abandoned locations is situated? And, if possible, can you piece together the exact location?

Abandoned: 1986
Population exodus:
49,400

_____

_____

Location type:
Amusement park
Abandoned: 2005
Reason: Natural
disaster

_____

_____

**3**

Abandoned: 2003
Condition: Mortar damage and gunfire. Traces of former grand opulence.

_____

_____

**4**

Building type: Houses reclaimed by the desert
Clues found: Raw diamonds and a German flag beneath the sand

_____

_____

**5**

Building type: Abandoned nitrate mining town
Abandoned: 1960
Located: In the world's driest desert

_____

_____

# GLOBAL GEOGRAPHY QUIZ

Global geography plays such a huge role in the interplay between countries that sometimes its significance can be lost amid the political intrigue and discord, financial systems and structures, and religious worship. Test yourself with this quiz to sharpen your geographical knowledge.

1. The surface of the Earth is approximately 70.9% water and 29.1% land. The majority of the Earth's surface is made up of five oceans. Can you arrange these oceans, listed below, in size order, starting with the largest?

Arctic, Atlantic, Indian, Pacific, Southern

_____

_____

_____

_____

_____

2. Considering there are five oceans, how might the world's oceans end up as the "Seven Seas"?

_____

_____

3. What percentage of the Earth's water is saltwater?

☐ 74%     ☐ 62.5%     ☐ 97.5%     ☐ 86%

4. What catastrophic geographical occurrence would cause sea levels to rise by 230 feet, and why?

_____

_____

_____

5. Can you explain what is being shown in the graphic below?

_____

_____

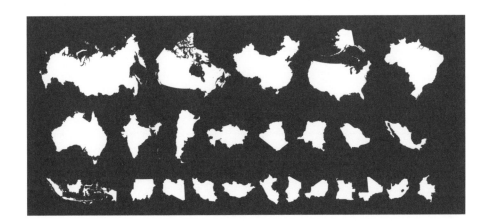

# INTERNATIONAL AFFAIRS

6. Parts of five countries lie in both Europe and Asia. Can you name the countries?

7. Which two countries that lie entirely in western Asia are geopolitically defined as European?

8. What is the longest mountain range in the world? And which seven countries (the first of which is rich in oil reserves) does it span?

9. What totals 156,001 miles in length and can be a source of international disputes and refugee crises, and is heavily controlled?

10. At which waterfall would you find the "Devil's Throat"?

11. What canal links the Red Sea with the Mediterranean Sea?

12. The circum-Pacific belt, highlighted on the map below, is often referred to as "the Ring of Fire." What is it?

_____

_____

_____

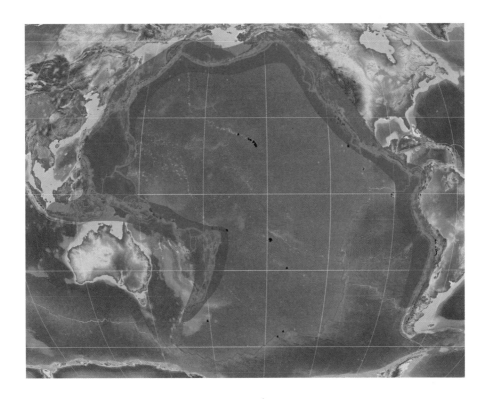

# SCRAMBLED CAPITAL CITIES

Unscramble these names of capital cities.

1. SRCAACA

_____

2. ÁBOTGO

_____

3. UNOBES SEARI

_____

4. GANATIOS

_____

5. RAJOSVAE

_____

6. AVANAH

_____

7. RAJAKAT

_____

8. ADMISLABA

_____

9. NEBRLI

_____

10. SPARI

_____

11. SRAWAW

_____

12. MOKOTCHLS

_____

13. KALUA PRULUM

_____

14. COMOWS

_____

15. SEULO

_____

16. OCRIA

_____

17. REBANCRA

_____

18. NIBAIRO

_____

# WHERE ARE YOU? RIVERS

Can you work out the countries that are home to each of the rivers shown in these satellite images?

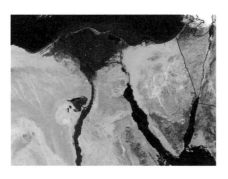

1. _____

2. _____

3. _____

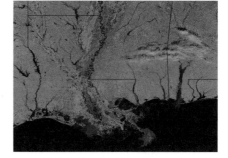

4. _____

# STARS

Can you identify the country from the formation of stars on its flag?

1. _____

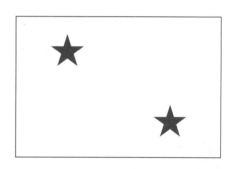

2. _____

3. _____

4. _____

5. _____

6. _____

7. _____

8. _____

9. _____

10. _____

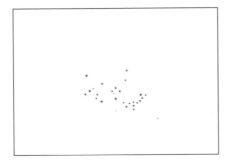

11. _____

12. _____

# COCKTAIL MENU

You must take a journey across the world. In each place you will be given details of the surveillance operation you must undertake and intelligence you must gather. You are given a coded list of the countries you must visit, which you pick up from a bartender at a cocktail bar. The name of each country is given to you in its etymological form (e.g., the origins of the country's name) via the name of each cocktail. A short description of the cocktail offers a clue. Plot the course of your mission on the map below. The countries have been highlighted for you, but no names have been provided. Match the entomological cocktails to the country, and plot the course of your mission.

## Cocktail Menu

1. Land Beside the Silvery River
(Think silvery French notes)

2. Bearded Ones (Rum-based)

3. The Savior (This tequila martini is literally divine)

4. Free (Bourbon and rum)

5. Land of the Many Rabbits (Sherry-based)

6. The Land of Honey (Malt whisky and honey)

7. Light Stone (Asbach cognac gives this a German flavor)

8. White Russia (Beautiful white vodka)

9. Land of the Indus River (Spicy mango daiquiri)

10. I Go to the Beach (The world's smallest cocktail)

## COUNTRIES ON MISSION ROUTE:

1. _____
2. _____
3. _____
4. _____
5. _____

6. _____
7. _____
8. _____
9. _____
10. _____

# HUMAN GEOGRAPHY QUIZ

The world is a melting pot of cultures, religions, and demographics. Tensions can arise whenever any of these human factors is tested or cultures clash. With this in mind, test your knowledge of global human geography.

1. Below is a table showing the populations of the top ten most populous countries in the world.
(Figures 2017 est. in millions).

Provided are the names of twelve countries. Can you firstly identify the ten most populous countries? And secondly, can you put them in the correct order in the table?

Bangladesh
Brazil
Canada
China
India
Indonesia
Japan
Nigeria
Pakistan
Russia
Somalia
United States

| Population | |
|---|---|
| 1,379 | |
| 1,282 | |
| 327 | |
| 261 | |
| 207 | |
| 205 | |
| 191 | |
| 158 | |
| 142 | |
| 126 | |

2. Collectively, more than a third of the world's population inhabits which two countries?

_____

3. In terms of statistics, what links Macau and Greenland? Clue: they are opposite ends of the scale.

_____

_____

4. What four languages would you have to learn to converse with over a quarter of the world's population in their first language?

_____

_____

5. Of the approximate 7,100 languages spoken in the world, how many are spoken by fewer than 10 people?

☐ 1   ☐ 15   ☐ 150   ☐ 1,500

6. What are the four most prevalent religions in the world?

_____

_____

7. What is the average salary (GDP per capita) when the figures from all the world's nations are calculated?

☐ $6,000
☐ $17,500
☐ $23,500
☐ $35,000

8. The opiate trade is a key source of revenue for the Taliban in Afghanistan. What percentage of the global heroin trade derives from Afghanistan?

☐ 10%
☐ 26%
☐ 63%
☐ 82%

# HUMAN DISPLACEMENT

The displacement of peoples can cause immense pain and suffering, and can lead to massive geopolitical tensions and humanitarian crises. This can have an impact both within the countries hosting refugees and the wider world, with political and economic ramifications. It is important to maintain a watchful eye on the key areas of human migration and hosting countries. Looking at the map below, can you name the ten countries that are host to more than half of the world's refugees and concentrated in the East African and Middle Eastern regions?

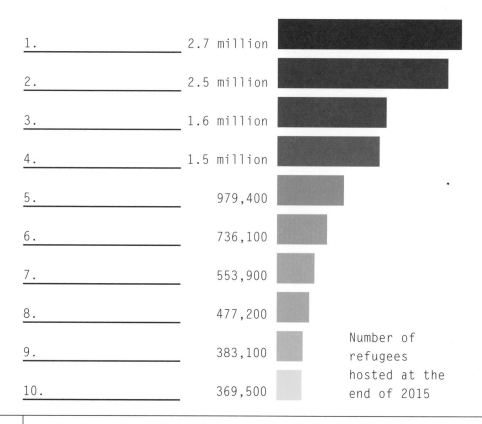

1. _____ 2.7 million

2. _____ 2.5 million

3. _____ 1.6 million

4. _____ 1.5 million

5. _____ 979,400

6. _____ 736,100

7. _____ 553,900

8. _____ 477,200

9. _____ 383,100

10. _____ 369,500

Number of refugees hosted at the end of 2015

# GEO-ECONOMICS AND CRUDE OIL

Crude oil is the source of many conflicts and geopolitical strategies. Its supply and consumption is crucial to every country on Earth. Without it the modern world cannot function. Observation of international affairs in the context of oil must be maintained. Some knowledge of the geo-economics of the world's leading sources and suppliers is vital. Below is a map of the world's leading oil-producing countries. Study the map and answer the questions relating to it.

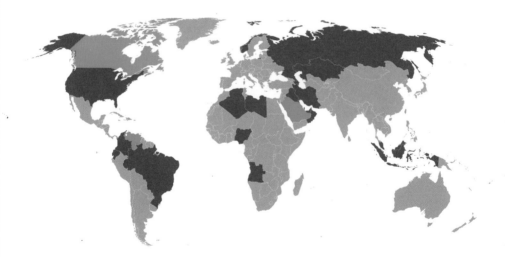

1. Which three countries, highlighted in red, have the largest oil reserves?

2. Which country leads the world in oil reserves yet is not in the top ten of oil producers?

_____

3. Which African country produces approximately 2,500,000 barrels of oil per day (the biggest producer in Africa) and is the 13th-largest oil producer in the world?

_____

4. Put these countries, which form the top five oil-producing countries in the world, in order (largest first).

Iraq, Iran, Russia, Saudi Arabia, United States

_____

_____

_____

_____

5. Which country uses 1.85 billion barrels of oil per day, more than any other country in the world?

_____

6. 99% of which country's oil exports go to the United States?

_____

7. OPEC is an international cartel comprising 14 oil-producing countries. It was founded in 1960 by five countries. Four are listed below; can you name the fifth?
Iraq, Kuwait, Saudi Arabia, Venezuela, ?

_____

8. Two major factors that contribute to the price of crude oil are supply and demand. What is considered the third major factor?
A. Climate
B. Geopolitics

_____

# GEO-ECONOMIC DEPENDENCIES: UNITED STATES

In the modern world, conflict between nations is played out as much through the intricacies of geopolitics and economics as on the battlefield. A world power can influence another country's political and military aims and policies by creating an economic dependency. This might be through trade deals and aid. As an agent, you must have an understanding of these intricacies. Below is a doughnut chart showing the top five recipients of U.S. foreign aid in terms of average dollars received per member of the population. Provided are the countries that make up this top five. Can you put them in the correct order, largest recipient first?

AFGHANISTAN
ISRAEL
JORDAN
LEBANON
WEST BANK/GAZA

1. _____

2. _____

3. _____

4. _____

5. _____

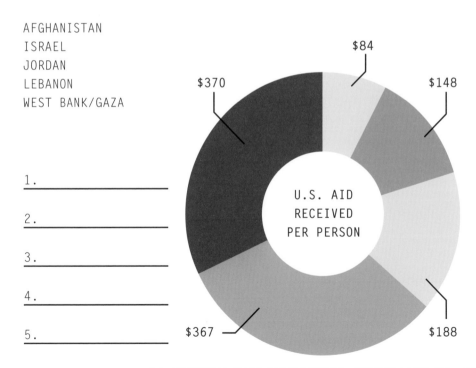

$370    $84    $148

U.S. AID
RECEIVED
PER PERSON

$367    $188

# GEO-ECONOMIC DEPENDENCIES: CHINA

Provided are the top ten exporters to China as measured by percentage of their overall exports. Can you place them in the correct order?

AUSTRALIA
BRAZIL
CHILE
INDONESIA
SOUTH KOREA
LEBANON
MALAYSIA
PERU
TAIWAN
THAILAND

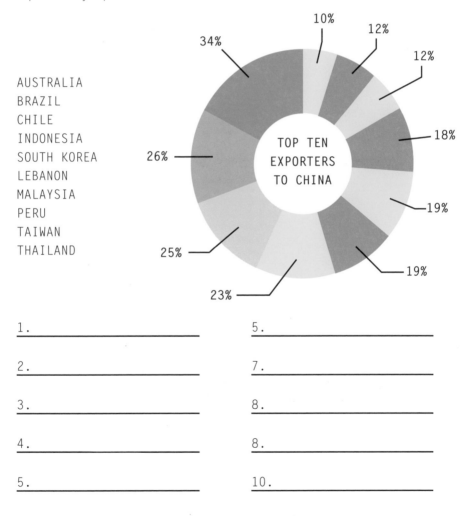

1. _____

2. _____

3. _____

4. _____

5. _____

5. _____

7. _____

8. _____

8. _____

10. _____

# THE ONLINE BATTLEFIELD

The grids below represent the potential online population of two of the world's great economic powers, the United States and China. Populations can be heavily influenced by what they see, and what they are allowed to see, online. Each segment of the grid equates to 15 million people. How much of each country's population grid would you shade in to represent the online population, and how much would you leave off-line?

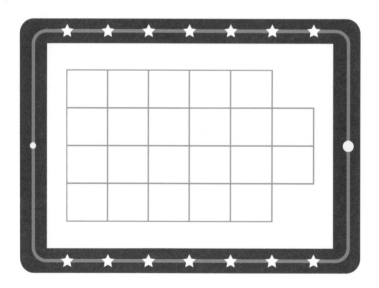

U.S. population = 324 million

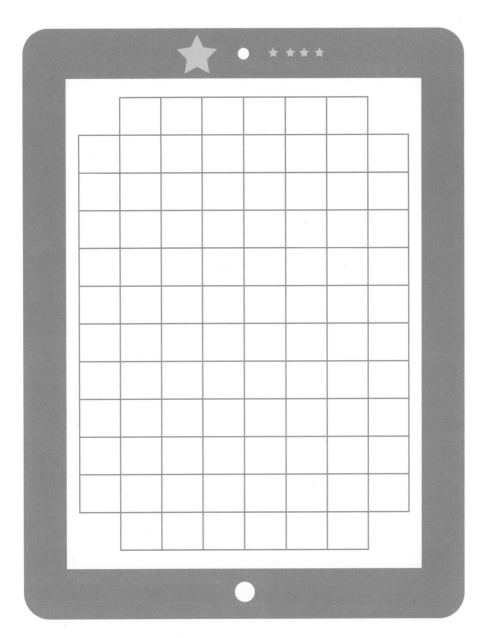

China population = 1,379 million

# TERRORIST GROUPS

The war on terror is an important part of CIA operations. As an agent, you must be able to identify terrorist organizations. Below and on the facing page are twelve flags of organizations designated terrorist groups by the United Nations. Match each terrorist group to its flag.

Hezbollah, Al-Qaeda in the Islamic Maghreb, Harkat ul Mujahideen, Al-Qaeda in Iraq, Eastern Indonesian Mujahideen, Jamiat-e Islami, Lashkar-e-Jhangvi, Islamic Jihad Movement in Palestine, Turkistan Islamic Party, New People's Army of the Philippines, Ansaru, Jaish-e-Mohammed

1. _____

3. _____

2. _____

4. _____

5. _____

6. _____

7. _____

8. _____

9. _____

10. _____

11. _____

12. _____

# MEMORY
# AND
# PERCEPTION

# MENTAL SELF-ROTATION

Follow the path of arrows from A to B, counting the number of left and right turns. Do not turn the page, use your hands, nor use any other guides. You must only imagine yourself moving within the location while counting the turns. This is a useful skill for map reading, negotiating complex circuit schematics, and general perception within an unknown environment.

1.

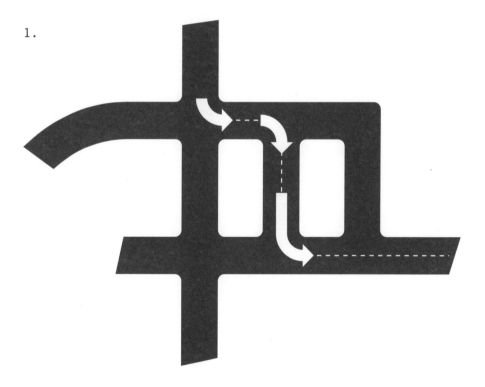

2.

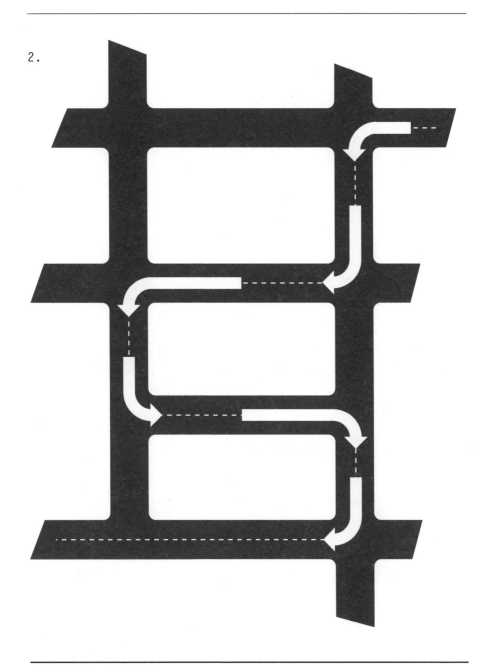

3.

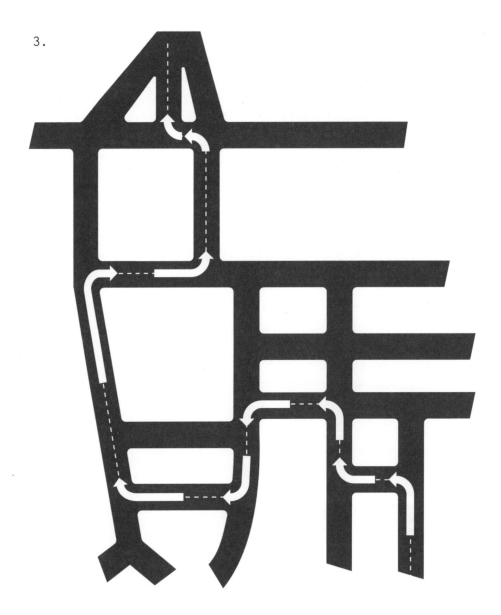

4.

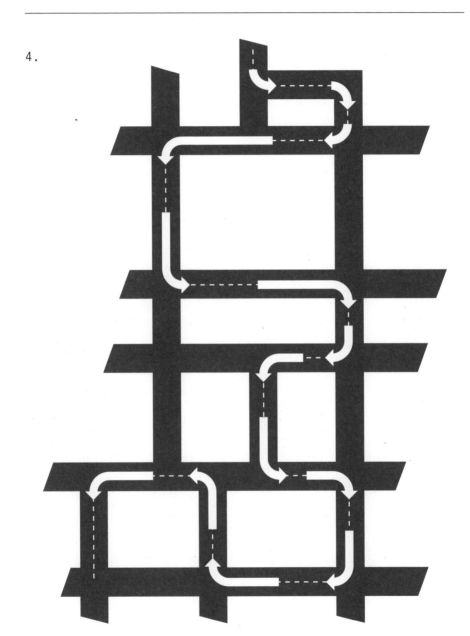

# SPOT THE DIFFERENCES

It is essential to be able to spot minor changes to an environment. Perception and instinct for things that just do not look right is key in the field. A building which has been amended in some way, or items shifted about or disappearing, can be a potential red light for suspicious activities. Can you spot the five changes in the photos below and opposite?

# SOMETHING ODD

Can you say what, if anything, appears odd about the following snippets of text?

1. The quick brown fox jumped over the lazy dog.

---

---

2. A gap will yawn, achingly, day by day, it will turn into a colossal pit, an abyss without foundation, a gradual invasion of words by margins, blank and insignificant, so that all of us, to a man, will find nothing to say.
(Source: Georges Perec, *La Disparition*, 1969)

---

---

3. Enfettered, these sentences repress free speech. The text deletes selected letters. We see the revered exegete reject metred verse
(Source: Christian Bök: Excerpts from *Eunoia*, 2009)

---

---

4. If you walk into the front *h*allway of the CIA, you will see, on your left, a statue of William "Wild Bill" Donovan. Bill Donovan was t*h*e person who created t*h*e OSS, t*h*e Office of Strategic Services, w*h*ich was America's spy agency during World War II and t*h*en kind of morp*h*ed into w*h*at's now the CIA.
David Ignatius
*"The Director" Offers a Glimpse into the Digital Underground*
June 3, 2014, 3:28 AM ET, Heard on *Morning Edition*

---

---

5. Heather's mother has four children, sons Mark, Marcus, and Michael. What is her fourth child called?

---

---

# FINDING THE ERROR

Sometimes an error can be glaringly obvious, and at other times can be harder to spot. Can you spot the the mistake on this page?

10  20  30  40
50  60  70  80
90  100

LINE A IS LONGER THAN LINE B

8 + 96 = 104

If the Mountain Time Zone is 1 hour ahead of the Pacific Time Zone, and the Central Time Zone is 1 hour ahead of the Mountain Time Zone, then the Central Time Zone is 2 hours ahead of the Pacific Time Zone.

LINE A          LINE B

ROTATED
45 DEGREES =

# HOW MANY HOLES?

How many holes are there in this sweater?

# MORNING, NOON, OR NIGHT?

What time of the day is it in the four photos? You might want to look at the details of any shadows, the direction of sunlight, and search for any other clues.

**1.**
☐ 7:00 a.m.
☐ 3:30 p.m.
☐ 7:00 p.m.

**2.**
☐ 8:30 a.m.
☐ 12:00 p.m.
☐ 4:00 p.m.

**3.**
- ☐ 7:30 a.m.
- ☐ 3:30 p.m.
- ☐ 6:30 p.m.

**4.**
- ☐ 7:00 a.m.
- ☐ 3:30 p.m.
- ☐ 8:00 p.m.

# RANDOM ICONS

Observe the icons on the page below and opposite and answer the accompanying questions. Can you answer each question within one minute?

1. The icons on each page are different except for one exact matching pair. Find the pair that are the same in every way.

2. One of the icons on the left page is the same as one on the right, except for a difference in size. Find the large and small corresponding icons.

3. One of the icons on the left page is the same as one on the right, except one of them has been rotated 180 degrees. Find the rotated icon.

# AIRDROP

A drone has been sent out to survey the rural scene below for an airdrop site. An agent is in the area and has been sent the schematic, together with the specific location for the drop in the form of a detached segment. The schematic segment has been rotated to avoid clear detection. Where is the drop to take place?

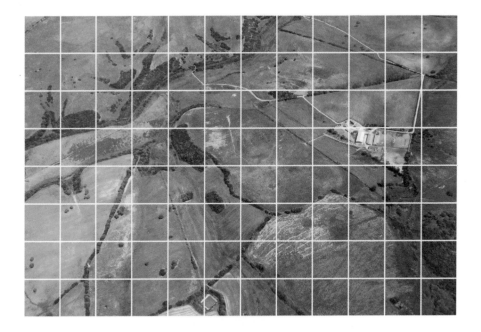

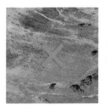

ROTATED
SEGMENT

# PRISON BREAK

A local informant has passed on information about the whereabouts of a doctor who was instrumental in the capture of a high-profile terrorist leader. The doctor is being held in a prison block. You have been given aerial images of the prison and must work out its schematics. You know that both blocks are divided into four cells per block. Every cell within each block is identical in shape and size. Doors on the left side access all the cells of the square block, with each cell connected by a wall. The location of doors on the L block is unknown. With this information, can you create a schematic of both prison blocks and help to rescue the doctor?

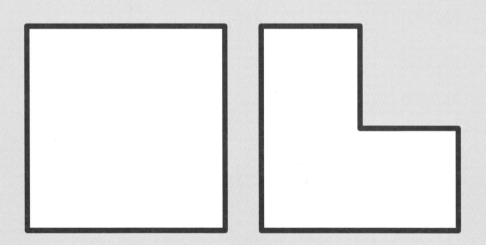

# SURVEILLANCE RISK

You must make your way across Berlin but are aware that your movements may be tracked. Certain routes across the city make it easier to avoid detection, whereas others are more open to being tracked. You have four possible routes, all varying in distance. A surveillance risk factor has been calculated for each of the four routes.

You also know that the longer you take to reach your destination, the greater the chance of being tracked. You must work out the best route to take from the information and map you have been given. Which route do you take?

| Route | Distance | Risk factor |
|-------|----------|-------------|
| Blue | 3.7 miles | 2.5 |
| Red | 3.5 miles | 3 |
| Green | 4 miles | 2.25 |
| Yellow | 4.6 miles | 2 |

BEST ROUTE:

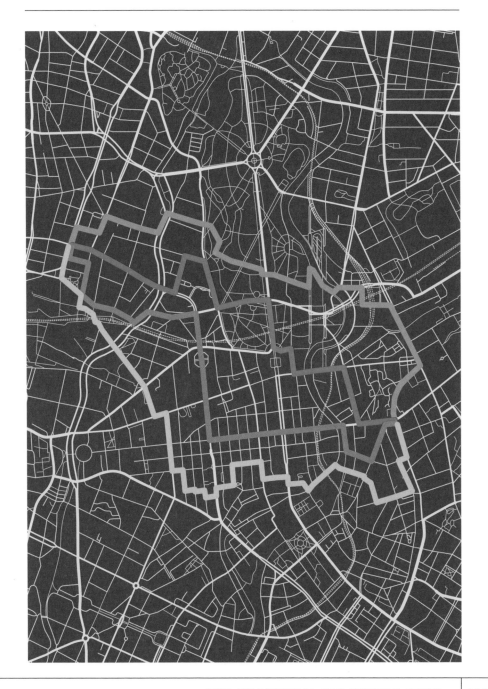

# FLAG CONNECTIONS

Which one of the flags below is the odd one out and why?

Zambia

Ecuador

Montenegro

Papua New Guinea

Dominica

# THE MIRROR TEST

1. Imagine you are standing 6 feet away from a mirror hanging flat on a wall directly in front of you. What is the shortest possible height the mirror must be to enable you to see your entire body in it? And where should it be positioned on the wall?

2. Imagine you are looking in a vertical mirror hanging flat on the wall, in which you can see the top half of your body, including your face, but cannot see your body below your knees. If you begin to step backward away from the mirror, are you able to:

- ☐ A. see more of your body?
- ☐ B. less of your body?
- ☐ C. the same amount of your body?

USE THIS SPACE FOR YOUR WORKINGS

# ENEMY LOCATION

A spy plane has taken aerial images of a group of buildings that are possibly being used as a base for a suspected terrorist cell. Similar buildings have been located previously. All have had the same structural characteristics. You have been tasked to draw up a basic layout of the buildings based on the information you have. You know the buildings consist of a basic two-room setup, and that a large wall separates the two. These rooms are always identical in shape to one another. The wall that divides them is never straight. With this information in hand, can you draw the location of the wall in each of the templates of the buildings opposite?

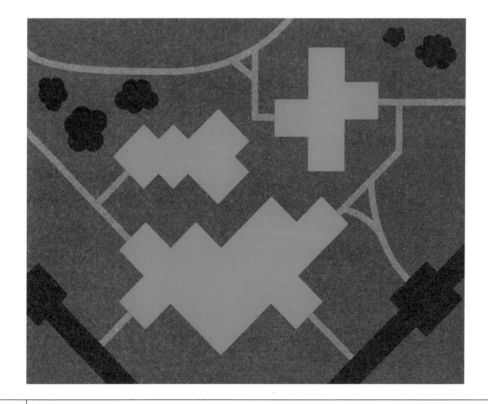

1.

2.

3.

# RANDOM OBJECTS MEMORY TEST

As a secret agent, you must develop the ability to memorize information given to you in a fleeting moment. You must be able to make snapshots in your mind, recording points of interest and suspicion. These might be a simple number plate of a vehicle you must track, an address given to you quickly and unrepeated, or an overheard piece of information of great importance.

Remembering playing cards is a classic way to begin learning memory techniques. The 12 face cards in a deck of 52 can easily be seen as having their own characters and so are a good starting point to the skill of memorizing things via visualization. Memory techniques are about assigning visual prompts to letters and numbers. In a standard pack of international casino cards, the king of hearts might be Frank Sinatra; the queen of diamonds, Marilyn Monroe. The jack of clubs, your Uncle Jarvis. The same technique can then be applied to every other card in the pack, such as the ace of spades being an "ace" pilot in a black flight suit. When you are then presented with a series of cards to memorize, you remember the sequence as a story or journey within a place that is well known to you, such as the city you live in, or your home. So you greet Frank Sinatra at the front door, pass Marilyn Monroe in the hallway, sit next to your Uncle Jarvis at the dining table, and invite the ace pilot to join you. This visual story is then easy to recall, and with it the sequence of cards.

Did you spot the number on the queen of diamonds? What was it?

Try taking this visualization technique and applying it to numbers and letters. A great method is to assign visual prompts that rhyme with the numbers 1 to 10. You can do the same with letters at a later stage.

| | | | | |
|---|---|---|---|---|
| 1 = BUN | 3 = TREE | 5 = BEEHIVE | 7 = HEAVEN | 9 = LINE |
| 2 = SHOE | 4 = DOOR | 6 = STICKS | 8 = GATE | 10 = HEN |

Object number 1 is a plane, so you might imagine a miniature plane landing on top of a bun (the more random the image, the easier it can be to recall). When you are asked to remember object number 1, the image will be clear in your mind. Once you reach object number 11, you must double up on the imagery (e.g., object number 11 is a star, and so you would go back to your bun, and perhaps imagine a miniature plane with a star painted on its side).

Have a look at the objects below and try to remember them using your visualization technique.

| | | | |
|---|---|---|---|
| 1 = ✈ | 6 = 💣 | 11 = ★ | 16 = ❄ |
| 2 = ✏ | 7 = 📖 | 12 = ☠ | 17 = ☎ |
| 3 = 💾 | 8 = 🔪 | 13 = 🖊 | 18 = 🕯 |
| 4 = 🗝 | 9 = ✂ | 14 = ✉ | 19 = ⏳ |
| 5 = 🔫 | 10 = 🔔 | 15 = ✿ | 20 = 👓 |

# MEMORY AND PERCEPTION

Answer the following questions relating to the objects on the previous page.

1. What objects are numbers 2, 4, and 7?

2. Which of these objects is not shown on the list?

☐ A.           ☐ B.           ☐ C.

3. Which object comes after number 8?

4. What comes after this object?

5. What objects are numbers 4 and 14?

6. Which of these objects is not shown on the list?

☐ A.           ☐ B.           ☐ C.

7. List numbers 1-10

8. List numbers 11-20

_____

_____

_____

_____

_____

_____

_____

_____

_____

9. What number is showing on the upturned corner of the queen of diamonds playing card?

_____

# MEMORIZING NUMBERS:
## VEHICLE REGISTRATION PLATES

The same memory technique used to recall a sequence of objects can be used to recall letters and numbers. This may be a vehicle registration plate, an address, or a coded message.

Assign a visual prompt for each of the 26 letters of the alphabet. A, B, and C have already been assigned but can be changed.

A - **AMAZON**

B - **BACON**

C - **COFFEE**

D -

E -

F -

G -

H -

I -

J -

K -

L -

M -

N -

O -

P -

Q -

R -

S -

T -

U -

V -

W -

X -

Y -

Z -

When remembering numbers, it can be useful to "chunk" them. Chunking is a memory technique whereby you break down a longer sequence into chunks. For example, 739281 would be remembered as 73 92 81. If you have a particular affinity for remembering events, either in your own life or famous historical events, then you can use these as number prompts. For example, you might assign the Falklands War to '82 or Lenin for '19 (Russian Revolution). You can assign a visual historical prompt for every number/year up to 100. So for example, 12827297 might end up as:

12: Titanic (the year the famous vessel sank in the Atlantic ocean, having hit an iceberg)
82: Falklands (the Falklands War of 1982)
72: Munich (the Olympic Games in which Israeli athletes were held hostage by Palestinian terrorists)
97: Hong Kong (ceded to China from UK in 1997)

These may seem either very random or may strike a chord. Your own prompts may well be random, but they will strike a chord with you and cement the numbers in your mind. When a series of numbers is read out, you may think of your Aunt May (born in '58) standing next to Neil Armstrong (set foot on the Moon in '69) attempting to eat a 72-oz. steak! (586972).

Below is a series of international vehicle registration plates. Spend some time trying to memorize these, using the techniques discussed, before turning the page.

| CH 182 747 | GB 746 912 |
| C 14 837 27 | DK 9988 76 |
| ZW 27 843 D | PK 64 7 29A |

# MEMORY AND PERCEPTION

Complete the international vehicle registration plates from the previous page, below:

1.

2.

3.

4.

5.

6.

# SECRET SERVICE CODE NAMES

U.S. presidents and their families have been given code names by the Secret Service since the beginning of the twentieth century. Code names have since been given to places, locations, and even objects, such as *Air Force One* and the presidential state car.

Can you find ways to memorize the Secret Service code name for each of the following people, locations, and objects? You might like to visualize them in the context of the code name. For example, imagine the presidential motorcade (code name BAMBOO) to be made out of bamboo. Or perhaps *Air Force One* (code name ANGEL) with angel wings instead of conventional aircraft wings. Give yourself some time to memorize these code names before covering them up and testing yourself. Can you return to these pages the next day and confirm you have committed them to memory?

| | |
|---|---|
| The presidential motorcade | – BAMBOO |
| Camp David | – CACTUS |
| The vice president's office | – COBWEB |
| The vice president's staff | – PACEMAKER |
| The Waldorf Astoria Hotel, New York City | – ROADHOUSE |
| Air Force One | – ANGEL |
| The U.S. presidential state car | – STAGECOACH |
| The White House | – CASTLE |
| The Capitol | – PUNCH BOWL |
| The White House Situation Room | – CEMENT MIXER |
| The Pentagon | – CALICO |
| Washington Dulles International Airport | – CURBSIDE |

# SPOT THE DIFFERENCE

Can you spot the four changes that have been made to each of these various types of transportation?

**ARE YOU SMART ENOUGH TO BE A SECRET AGENT?**

# X-RAY OBSERVATION

Observe the X-ray image of a backpack and its contents, below, for one minute before looking at the next page.

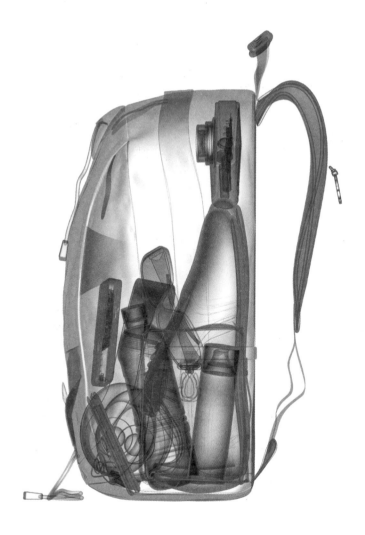

Observe the backpack once again, shown with a different orientation below. Which object has been removed from inside the backpack?

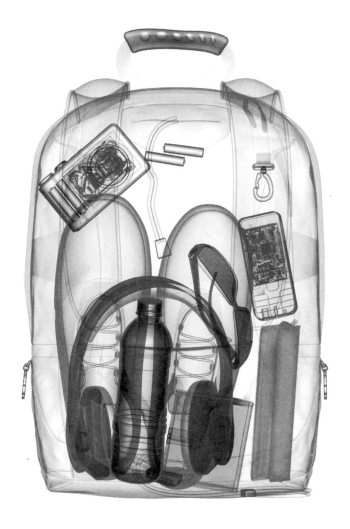

# QUICK PERCEPTION TESTS

Mental agility and superfast perception are vital skills for operatives to develop and constantly enhance. Complete these quick perception tests to sharpen your instincts, awareness, and observation.

1. Which of the boxes is shown in its template form opposite?

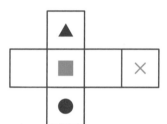

_____

A        B        C        D        E

2. Which one of these red circles is bigger?

_____

A                B

3. How many circles can you see here?

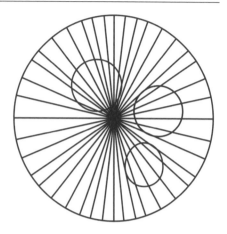

_____

4. Which takes up more of the other's area: the circle inside the square, or the square inside the circle?

_____

5. What is this map showing?

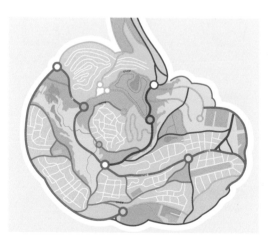

_____

# SAY WHAT YOU SEE

Often you will encounter things as an agent that are designed to distract, distort, and play with your perceptions. It is essential to have sharp instincts and responses to visual trickery. With minimal or no hesitation, and as quickly as possible, say what you see below out loud or in your head. There is a rule: when you see a square, you must say "circle," and when you see a circle, you must say "square." When you see a triangle, you must say "star," and when you see a star, you must say "triangle."

⬜ = CIRCLE     ◯ = SQUARE

△ = STAR     ☆ = TRIANGLE

◯   △   ⬜   ☆   △

⬜   △   ⬜   ◯   ⬜

☆   ◯   △   ◯   ☆

# MIRRORED NUMBERS?

Our minds are accustomed to seeing the world through a normal lens. When things are skewed in some way in an attempt to play with our natural perceptions, we must be mindful and aware, and adept at spotting them. A good test, and to hone sharpness, is to challenge the mind's instinct for mental rotation. The numbers below have been rotated randomly. Some are also represented as a mirror image of themselves. Observe each number in turn, and as quickly as possible determine whether they are of normal orientation or have been mirrored.

Tick the box next to the number if it has been mirrored.

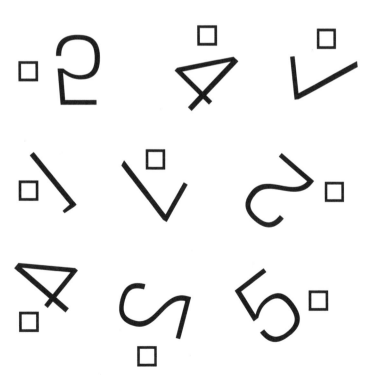

# WORLD
# HISTORY
# AND
# CONFLICT

# WHAT IS BEING SHOWN HERE?

Look at the series of pictograms below and on the following pages, each related in some way to the Cold War era. Can you work out what each one is showing?

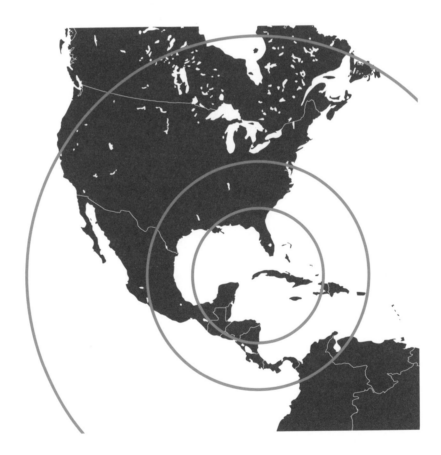

1. _____

Ich bin...

2. _____

3. _____

4. _____

5.

6.

# WEAPONS OF WAR

1. In which conflict of the twentieth century were chemical weapons used for the first time?
☐ Boer War (1899-1902)
☐ World War I (1914-1918)
☐ World War II (1939-45)
☐ Korean War (1950-1953)

2. What name was given to the project that developed the first nuclear bomb?
☐ The Manhattan Project
☐ The Staten Island Project
☐ The Bronx Project
☐ The Brooklyn Project

3. Which two countries supported the United States on the project?
☐ France and Switzerland
☐ Australia and South Africa
☐ UK and Canada
☐ Sweden and Holland

4. Which two Japanese cities were hit by nuclear bombs, killing between 129,000 and 226,000 people?
☐ Osaka and Narashi
☐ Kyoto and Neyagawa
☐ Hiroshima and Nagasaki
☐ Kobe and Kasugai

5. What name was given to the herbicide and defoliant chemical used by the United States in the Vietnam War between 1961 and 1971?
☐ Ranch Hand
☐ Agent X
☐ Agent Orange
☐ Rainbow H

6. What chemical was used to attack the Tokyo subway by a domestic terrorist group in 1995?
☐ Phosgene
☐ Mustard gas
☐ VX
☐ Sarin

# TECH

1. What was the name of the computer built by British codebreakers at Bletchley Park in 1943, one of the earliest electronic digital computers ever built?
☐ Colossus
☐ Hercules
☐ Trident
☐ Apollo

2. What cipher machines, invented in 1918, were used by the German navy before and during World War II to deliver coded messages?
☐ Scherbius
☐ Pegasus
☐ Enigma
☐ Geheimnis

3. In which year did Soviet astronaut Yuri Gagarin become the first person to travel into space?
☐ 1959
☐ 1961
☐ 1963
☐ 1965

4. The Strategic Defense Initiative was announced by U.S. president Ronald Reagan in 1983. What was it intended to do?
☐ Create a new branch of the special forces
☐ Build a nuclear submarine
☐ Create a nuclear bomb
☐ Develop a system to neutralize nuclear weapons

5. Under what name was the Strategic Defense Initiative project better known?
☐ Stargate
☐ Star Trek
☐ Star Wars
☐ Star Defense

6. What was the name of the first communication satellite sent into orbit by the United States in 1962?
☐ Explorer
☐ Sat 1
☐ Starlander
☐ Telstar 1

# WORLD LEADERS AT THE OUTBREAK OF WAR

Who were the leaders of the major world powers in the year each of the following conflicts began? Match the leaders shown on these pages to the countries they led at the start of each of the conflicts shown below.

Gerhard Schröder

## WORLD WAR I (1914)

Germany:_____

Russia:_____

UK:_____

United States:_____

Woodrow Wilson

## WORLD WAR II (1939)

Germany:_____

Russia:_____

UK:_____

United States:_____

Joseph Stalin

## 2ND IRAQ WAR (2003)

Germany:_____

Russia:_____

UK:_____

United States:_____

Adolf Hitler

Czar Nicholas II

Tony Blair

Vladimir Putin

Kaiser Wilhelm II

George W. Bush

Neville
Chamberlain

Franklin D.
Roosevelt

David Lloyd
George

# WITNESSES OF HISTORY

Look at the quotes below and identify the historical events they describe.

"... the person wished to grasp the President's hand in both his own. In the palm of one hand, the right one, was a handkerchief. Then there were two shots in rapid succession, the interval being so short as to be scarcely measurable. I stood stockstill."
*John D. Wells, reporter for the* Buffalo Morning Review, *1901*

1. What event is being described here?

_____

"I have never seen in any face such joy as radiated from the faces of the people of Paris this morning."
*Charles Christian Wertenbaker,* TIME*'s war correspondent, 1944*

2. What event is being described here?

_____

"I heard people... yelling, screaming, and crying... a wall had gone up overnight. Friends and relatives who had been visiting in East Berlin were now stuck and would not be allowed to return."
*Marion Cordon-Poole, American child staying with the family of her German mother in 1961*

3. What is being reflected upon here?

"I was walking up Howard Street in downtown Baltimore—I was still in uniform. A truck backfired about two blocks behind me. I just yelled, 'Incoming!' and hit the pavement. It just freaked everybody out. I said, 'To hell with this.' Next morning I took the bus, went down to the Pentagon and had orders changed to go back..."
*Michael Rosensweig, U.S. Army Rangers Specialist E-4*

4. Where is this soldier talking about returning to?

"I was near the airport at Da Nang when the city was liberated on March 29, 1975."
*Bui Thi Tron, Vietnam People's Army Corporal*

5. Which war is this army corporal talking about?

"I ask every citizen to reject the blind violence that has struck Dr. King, who lived by nonviolence."
*U.S. president Lyndon B. Johnson, 1968*

6. The aftermath of which event is being referenced here?

"That story... is not getting weaker because of time. Because we don't know who he is, it's actually getting stronger... In the long frame of history... human freedom, courage, dignity will stay and prevail, and that's what that picture will testify forever."
*Xiao Qiang, Editor-in-Chief of the* China Digital Times

7. What event was captured in the photograph this journalist is talking about?

"That's one small step for man, one giant leap for mankind."

8. What error was contained in the message received by ground control from Neil Armstrong when he stepped on the Moon in 1969, reportedly due to static interference?

# HISTORY IN NUMBERS

Answer each of the following questions with a number.

1. How many times was U.S. president Franklin D. Roosevelt elected (the most of any U.S. president)?

_____

2. In the political slogan adopted by Mao Zedong in 1956 to allow more freedom of speech in communist China, how many "Flowers Bloom"?

_____

3. Fill in the blank. In 1954 Vietnam was divided temporarily into North and South along a circle of latitude known as the ___th Parallel.

_____

4. Fill in the blank. Stalag ___ was a German prisoner-of-war camp during World War II.

_____

5. During World War II a message sent by a German Enigma cipher machine could be encrypted using approximately how many different possible settings?
☐ 15,000
☐ 15 million
☐ 15 billion
☐ 15 billion billion

# MAP OF CHANGE

1. What series of events that changed the face of Africa over a number of decades is represented by this map?

_____

_____

2. What do the years denote?

_____

_____

_____

3. What do the colors denote?

_____

_____

_____

1961

1922

1956

1960

1957

1960

1960

1975

1990

1961

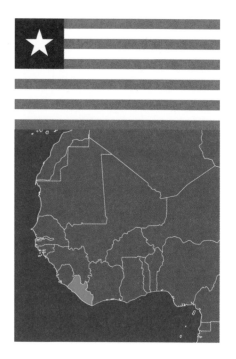
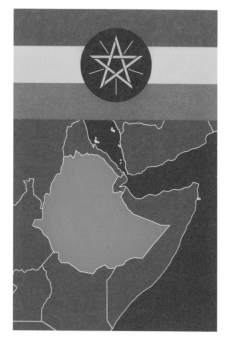

4. Which countries are represented in the maps above?

_____

5. What is unique about these countries in the context of the map on the previous page?

_____

_____

# FAMOUS FIRSTS

Match up these groundbreaking historical events with the years they occurred.

1967, 1893, 1973, 1868, 1839, 1963, 1903, 1911

1. Louis Daguerre takes the first photographic self-portrait (the first "selfie")

_____

2. Marie Curie becomes the first person to win two Nobel Prizes

_____

3. Thurgood Marshall becomes the first African American to become a U.S. Supreme Court justice

_____

4. New Zealand becomes the first country to give women the right to vote

_____

5. The first cell phone, a Motorola, is produced

_____

6. The first powered flight by the Wright brothers takes place at Kitty Hawk, North Carolina

_____

7. Russian cosmonaut Valentina Vladimirovna becomes the first woman in space

_____

8. First traffic lights are installed in Parliament Square, London

_____

# SPANNING THE GLOBE

At the bottom of the page are three countries that span the globe, from Mexico in North America, to Indonesia in Southeast Asia, to Egypt in North Africa. Each country has two facts relating to its recent history, shown below. Can you match the six facts to the three countries?

1. This country was known as the United Arab Republic from 1958 to 1971:

_____

2. In 1967 this country fought in the Six-Day War, one of the shortest wars ever recorded:

_____

3. In 1934 the restoration of the ancient Ejido system (establishing communally shared farmland) brought relative peace and stability to this country:

_____

4. This country ceded independence to East Timor in 2002:

_____

5. A civil war ravaged this country between 1910 and 1920, resulting in the deaths of over 2 million people:

_____

6. In 1949 this country used guerrilla warfare to successfully defeat the Dutch, who were attempting to reclaim control following World War II:

_____

MEXICO          INDONESIA          EGYPT

# MIXED-UP QUOTES

A colleague has been testing her encryption skills by taking a series of famous historical quotes, splitting them into groups, and mixing them up. She has asked you to rearrange the groups of letters so they fit together to make a coherent line of text, from where the original quote will become apparent. Can you help your colleague and reveal the four historical quotes?

1. KEOT SHAP LLMA VERI WHOE
YTOO HAPP PYWI HERS
—*Anne Frank*

_____

_____

2. NOTI MEWE EVER LING INRI
NLIV LLIN SING THEG ERFA
LORY FALL GBUT REAT ESTG
LIES NNEV YTI
—*Nelson Mandela*

_____

_____

_____

3. OURR NITA NGON HEEN IEAK
OURE NDHA NOTI OPET DOFY
ACHT WHENY
—*Franklin D. Roosevelt*

_____

_____

_____

4. ESF HENO SMAD THIS DOVE
TEUP RNEY RTHE DIMI WNES
IHAV EARS NISH MIND HATI
ELEA EAR
—*Rosa Parks*

_____

_____

_____

# HISTORICAL LINKS

What links these four major events of the twentieth century?

1962: The Cuban Missile Crisis brings the world to the brink of nuclear war

1929: The Wall Street crash hits America and the world

1923: The Republic of Turkey is created, with Atatürk as its first leader

1956: Start of the Second Arab-Israeli War triggers the Suez Crisis

# A TO Z QUIZ

1. What name is given to the joint army of Australia and New Zealand that fought at the Battle of Gallipoli in 1915-16?

A: _____

2. Which Tim invented the World Wide Web while at CERN in 1989?

B: _____

3. The Soviet Union violently crushed an attempted uprising in which country in 1968?

C: _____

4. The Battle of Jutland (1916) took place off the coast of which European country?

D: _____

5. Which U.S. president was knighted by the UK?

E: _____

6. Which military dictator ruled Spain from 1939 to 1975?

F: _____

7. Which Russian term meaning "openness and transparency" was popularized by Mikhail Gorbachev in the mid-1980s?

G:

8. Which Japanese emperor oversaw the killing of between 3 and 10 million people between 1937 and 1945?

H:

9. What name was given to the mass Palestinian uprising in the West Bank and Gaza Strip in 1987?

I:

10. This capital city, formerly known as Batavia, was renamed following Japanese occupation in 1942. What is its name?

J:

11. The 1934 Röhm Purge in Nazi Germany is better known as "The Night of the Long..."?

K:

12. Riots in which U.S. city were triggered following the brutal arrest of Rodney King in 1992?

L:

13. Which treaty formed the European Union in 1992?

M:

14. Which U.S. president was the first to visit China?

N: _____

15. Which theoretical physicist was instrumental in the development of the atomic bomb?

O: _____

16. What term was given to Soviet leader Mikhail Gorbachev's policy of reform in 1986?

P: _____

17. Which Canadian province underwent a "Quiet Revolution" in the 1960s?

Q: _____

18. On which island did future South African president Nelson Mandela spend most of his 27-year prison term?

R: _____

19. In which country was Sirimavo Bandaranaike elected as the world's first female prime minister in 1960?

S: _____

20. The name of which offensive of the Vietnam War was named for the Vietnamese New Year holiday?

T: _____

21. Boris Yeltsin Peak is a mountain in which Russian mountain range, renamed in 2002 after the first president of the Russian Federation?

U:

22. In which country did Hugo Chávez lead the "Bolivarian Revolution"?

V:

23. In which Texas city did a 51-day siege end with the killing of cult leader David Koresh and 70 of his followers?

W:

24. Wilhelm Röntgen won the 1901 Nobel Prize in Physics for the discovery of what?

X:

25. What slogan was used by the Khmer Rouge to signify the start of their rule of terror in Cambodia in 1975? "_____ Zero"

Y:

26. Who was king of Albania from 1928 to 1939?

Z:

# ODD ONE OUT

Which of these is not a true code name assigned to a military operation?

**A. BARBAROSSA**
German invasion of the Soviet Union in 1941.

**B. DESERT STORM**
A U.S.-led allied offensive against Iraqi targets in 1991.

**C. FREQUENT WIND**
The U.S. evacuation of Saigon, Vietnam, in 1975.

**D. MINCEMEAT ("the man that never was")**
A deception by the British military to disguise the allied invasion of Sicily in 1943. A recently deceased homeless man was dressed as a Royal Marine, with a letter suggesting Sardinia was the target, and floated out to sea for the Germans to find (it worked!).

**E. MONGOOSE**
An operation by the Kennedy administration in 1961 to overthrow Cuban leader Fidel Castro.

**F. OVERLORD**
Code name for the allied invasion of German-occupied Western Europe, launched with the Normandy landings, 1944.

**G. RAWHIDE**
A security operation undertaken by the military following the attempted assassination of U.S. president Ronald Reagan in 1981.

# PICTURE QUIZ

Who are these twentieth-century historical figures?

1.

2.

3.

4.

5.

6.

7.

8.

9.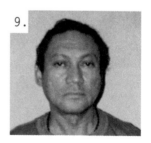

# FIND THE LINK

Can you find what links the entries in the three lists below, adding a fifth entry to each list?

Liberia = Joseph Jenkins Roberts, 1847
Russian Federation = Boris Yeltsin, 1991
Argentina = Manuel Belgrano, 1816
Republic of Singapore = Lee Kuan Yew, 1965
United States of America = ?

Battle of Waterloo, 1815
Battle of Yalu River, 1904
Second Battle of the Masurian Lakes, 1915
Battle of Cape Matapan, 1942
?

Greece, 1821-29
Estonia, 1918-20
Ireland, 1919-21
Croatia, 1991-95
?

# UNSCRAMBLE

Unscramble these sets of letters to reveal the surnames of famous military generals.

1. MELROM

2. CFPARHWOKSZ

3. REWENISHOE

4. RAATHCRUM

5. COFRAN

6. AREVAGU

Unscramble these sets of letters to reveal the names of famous twentieth-century scientists.

7. CRIDHAR NENFMAY

8. TRLEAB INENSITE

9. MAIER ECUIR

10. GUDINMS FUDRE

11. VANI VAVLOP

12. RODALINS KLIFNNAR

# COLD WAR TIMELINE

The geopolitical tensions of the Cold War between 1947 and 1991 resulted in some major incidents and events between the opposing factions of East and West. Below are some of the key incidents from this period. Each one is incomplete. Can you find the missing words?

1. 1945: The Yalta _____ is held to decide the fate of Germany.

2. 1948: A communist coup d'état, with Soviet backing, takes place in the eastern European nation of _____.

3. 1949: The Berlin _____ thwarts a Soviet attempt to starve the people of West Berlin into submission.

4. 1950: The _____ War begins with the United States and Soviet Union backing opposing sides.

5. 1955: The Soviet Union and seven of its satellite states sign a treaty, forming a collective, known as the _____ Pact

6. 1957: Laika the _____ is the first living creature sent into orbit, a key moment in the "Space Race" between the United States and Soviet Union.

7. April 1961: The United States fails in the Bay of _____ invasion, an attempt to overthrow Fidel Castro's communist regime in Cuba.

8. August 1961: After the Berlin Wall went up, separating East and West Berlin, there is a standoff between U.S. and Soviet tanks on opposite sides of Checkpoint _____.

9. 1962: The world comes perilously close to nuclear war with the _____ Missile Crisis.

10. 1968: Warsaw Pact forces enter Czechoslovakia to quash the "Prague _____."

11. 1973: U.S. involvement in the Vietnam War ends with the _____ Peace Accords.

12. 1980: The United States boycotts the summer Olympics held in _____ as a protest against the Soviet invasion of Afghanistan.

13. 1989: The _____ Revolution leads to the end of Communist rule in Czechoslovakia.

# HISTORICAL SPEECHES

Can you work out the quotes taken from well-known historical speeches, hidden below?

1.
I
H _ _ _
A
D _ _ _ _

2.
I _ _
B _ _
E _ _
B _ _ _ _ _ _ _

3.
I
A _
P _ _ _ _ _ _ _
T _
D _ _

4.
T _ _
W _ _ _
O _
C _ _ _ _ _

5.
W _
W _ _ _
N _ _ _ _
S _ _ _ _ _ _ _ _

6.
T _ _
O _ _ _
T _ _ _ _
W _
H _ _ _
T _
F _ _ _
I _
F _ _ _
I _ _ _ _ _

# FIND THE MISSING NUMBERS

Complete the historical facts below by filling in the missing numbers.

1. The formal Japanese surrender aboard the USS *Missouri* (VJ Day) took place on ___/2/1945.

2. The start of Soviet-Afghan War was in 197__.

3. When a nuclear reactor went into partial meltdown at a nuclear power station in Pennsylvania in 1979, it was known as the __ Mile Island accident.

4. The Battle of Ypres in Belgium took place during World War __.

5. The Austro-Prussian War of 1866 was also known as the __ Weeks War.

6. In 1970 *Apollo* ___, the intended third Moon landing in the Apollo space program, was launched.

# DICTATORS AND DESPOTS

Match the dictators and despots, pictured, with the descriptions of their atrocities.

**1**
Pol Pot
(Cambodia)

**2**
Mao Zedong
(China)

**3**
Augusto Pinochet
(Chile)

**4**
Leopold II
(Belgium)

**5**
Saddam Hussein
(Iraq)

**6**
Idi Amin
(Uganda)

**A**

Ordered the mass genocide of Kurds, Shabaks, Assyrians, Mandeans, and any ethnic group that rebelled against him. He fought a long war with a neighboring country. Wars, invasions, and atrocities led to the deaths of approximately 2 million of his people.

**B**

Leader of the Khmer Rouge (1963–1997) who killed approximately 2.5 million people during his reign of genocide. Died from suspected suicide in 1998 after learning of his impending international tribunal.

**C**

Between 1949 and 1976, this Communist leader executed up to 6 million of his people, as well as numerous "enemies of the state." His policies arguably killed up to 20 million people via starvation.

**D**

This leader ruled his country between 1971–79. He is believed to have killed 100,000–500,000 people through ethnic prejudice and extrajudicial killings. He was initially seen as a freedom fighter and then a pro-Western ruler with large support from Israel, before shifting to alliances with Libya, Zaire, the Soviet Union, and East Germany.

**E**

Leader of a Latin American military junta state. He persecuted political enemies and executed up to 3,200 people, interned up to 80,000, and tortured tens of thousands. His rule ended in 1998, leaving a brutal legacy.

**F**

Colonial leader purported to have enslaved and killed nearly 15 million Congolese under the guise of his Congo Free State. He was initially seen by many as having liberated the Congolese from the Zanzibari Arab slave traders before his brutal colonial rule.

# TECHNIQUES

# INVISIBLE INK

Espionage often takes place in the most modest of places—a hotel lobby, a coffee shop, a station terminal. Messages can be passed on in the full light of day. One technique would be to use random and seemingly innocent items to hide a secret message.

Below, a hotel business card has been printed to hide a secret message. The message lies within the hotel's name and address as an anagram. Note that the number of letters in the address do not correspond with the number of letters in the hidden text. Can you decipher the hidden message?

**Abbey Hotel,**

Fork Sleeps Path, Rignore – England, UK

A-- T-- B--- B-- F-- T-- P-----

In a similar vein as the hotel business card on the previous page, a hotel's headed notepaper has been left by a guest who that morning has checked out of the room in which you are now staying. The headed paper has been used to pass on a secret message to be deciphered and acted upon. The hidden message is written in invisible ink, which you have revealed, and it must now be deciphered. Somewhere on the headed notepaper is text that will help to read the hidden message.

## Apostrophe Hotel, Rue de Chevreuse, Paris, France

"The Apostrophe Hotel is a 'Poem Hotel' in the 6th arrondissement of Paris, located on the left bank between Montparnasse and the Jardins du Luxembourg, close to Saint-Germain-des-Prés. Each room has a unique design based on a literary theme."

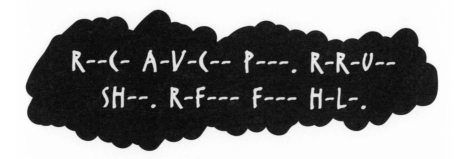

R--(- A-V-(-- P---. R-R-U-- SH--. R-F--- F--- H-L-.

# COINS AND BANKNOTES

Simple everyday objects such as coins and banknotes can be useful to a secret agent. They can be used to pass messages on, such as writing a message on a banknote and passing it over in an exchange of money without arousing suspicion. Coins can be useful in many ways. For one, you can always have a few in your pocket. A jangle of the coins in the pocket can act as a warning signal. Another way is to pass time away with some coin-based puzzles. This might sound like time-wasting, but in fact it can be very useful.

For example, in the period after a detainee has been broken after hours, days, even weeks of interrogation, it is essential to keep their mind from their own thoughts. Anything to keep them occupied and distracted can be very useful. An agent at this point, who has perhaps also been tasked with being a friendly face to the detainee, might use the coins in their pocket and some puzzles for some light relief and distraction. Here are three such puzzles to be solved on an "interrogation" table (a simple rectangular table with seven coins placed upon it).

1.The first is this. You have seven coins. Can you arrange these coins into six rows with three coins in each of the rows?

2. Using three coins, what is the farthest distance the coins can be apart from each other on the table while maintaining equal distance from one another?

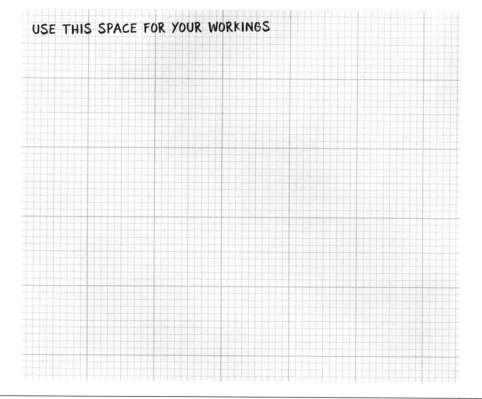

USE THIS SPACE FOR YOUR WORKINGS

# TECHNIQUES

3. Starting with the coins in the configuration shown in the uppermost diagram below, and moving only two adjacent coins at a time, can you create the configuration of coins in the second diagram in just three moves?

There are some rules:
1. Any gaps created when coins are moved cannot be closed by pushing coins together. Gaps can only be filled by moving two touching coins into them.
2. When two touching coins are moved, at least one of them has to end up touching another coin.
Note: The easiest way to maneuver two coins at a time is to slide them together on a table surface.

# 638 TECHNIQUES TO KILL CASTRO

There were a reported 638 attempts to assassinate the communist Cuban leader Fidel Castro during his 49 years in power.

Six of the following eight methods are true assassination attempts. Can you weed out the false two?

1. A lethal injection using a syringe hidden within a pen
2. Recruiting his wife as a contract-agent to poison him
3. Replacing one of his cigars with one laced with LSD
4. Poisoning his refrigerated milkshake
5. An exploding chess piece to be detonated during a game
6. Planting explosives in a large, exotically painted seashell to lure Castro when on a scuba dive
7. Contaminating Castro's scuba diving wet suit with a powerful fungus
8. Handing him a handkerchief covered in harmful bacteria and toxins

# THE INTERROGATION ROOM

In an interrogation scenario, every minor detail is considered. There are many techniques used to coax information from a detainee. The setup of the interrogation room itself is very important. In the picture opposite, can you spot the six errors in the layout of this interrogation room?

1. _____

2. _____

3. _____

4. _____

5. _____

6. _____

# MEALTIME?

Can you explain what interrogation trick is being used in the three pictures of a detainee's detention cell below? It is a method used by interrogators when they are trying to break a prisoner's resolve.

_____

_____

_____

_____

# CODED SHOELACES

During the Cold War the CIA released *The Manual of Trickery and Deception*. It was created to give agents various techniques that could be used during covert operations. It offered guidance for sleights of hand, using spy gadgets, and passing on secret messages to other agents. One such technique was to pass on messages via the pattern in which shoelaces were tied. This could be a way to alert danger, indicate receipt of an item such as documentation, or an agreed method of identification.

Using the templates opposite, create your own signals, bearing in mind the shoelaces would take time to untie and reconfigure, and would need to be done without arousing suspicion. What messages might you pass on?

SIGNAL          MESSAGE

O     O

O     O         _____

O     O         _____

O     O         _____

O     O

O     O         _____


O     O

O     O         _____

O     O         _____

O     O         _____

O     O

O     O         _____


O     O         _____

O     O         _____

O     O         _____

O     O         _____

O     O

O     O         _____

# CREATING SIGNALS

Other ways of passing on signals in *The Manual of Trickery and Deception* were via clothing, such as marked buttons on a blazer, and even a sweater with Morse code stitched into it.

These might be signaling:
I have the papers
I am being followed
The path is clear

Can you think of other, similar ways in which messages might be conveyed? Jot them down or draw a rough sketch opposite. For example, this might be the way in which a tie is knotted or hair coiffured.

USE THIS SPACE FOR YOUR OWN SIGNALS

# "WHAT IF" SCENARIOS

1. How were guard dogs dealt with, considering that all traces of an agent's presence should remain hidden?
☐ A. Sidestep them at all costs
☐ B. Shoot them, ensuring use of a gun silencer
☐ C. Use dog-calming commands
☐ D. Tranquilize with laced food and inject to resuscitate on exit

2. Suppose you are staying the night in a hotel located in an area of political turmoil, where a danger exists that insurgents might bomb the hotel. What item do you ensure is next to your bed above all else when you go sleep?
☐ A. A gun
☐ B. Your cell phone
☐ C. Your shoes
☐ D. A bulletproof vest

3. What if you are taken hostage? Of the four techniques described below, which one is not advised?
☐ A. Try to leave traces of blood in each location you find yourself so that your path can be traced.
☐ B. Pretend to be very ill so that your captors are less likely to want to hold you captive.
☐ C. Be very submissive and weak in the hope your captors let security lapse through complacency.
☐ D. Be very confident and imposing in the hope that your captors see you as a threat and are thus less likely to want to hold you captive.

# DEFUSING A BOMB

You are in a crisis situation. You have uncovered a bomb in the basement of an office building. It must be defused to avert disaster. You make a quick assessment of the bomb. It is a timed device with seven colored wires. Each wire connects matching nodes. The wires are designed to confuse. All seven wires cross one another. You have handled a similar device before. You know that only one of the wires has the capacity to connect matching nodes without crossing any other wires or nodes. It is this wire that must be cut to defuse the bomb. A bead of sweat drips to the floor from your brow as you see the timer on the device. You have under a minute to cut the wire and avert disaster. Which wire do you cut?

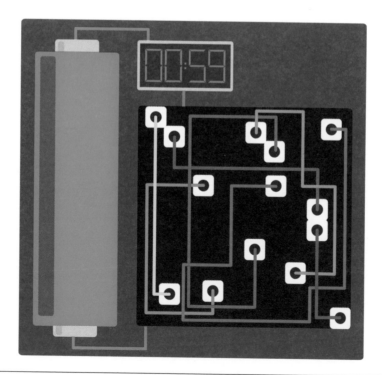

# COMPLEX CIPHERS

The complexity of ciphers varies from basic number-to-letter substitutions through to the cracking of the German Enigma code during World War II. Below is a columnar transposition cipher, which is a relatively complex method of encryption. You must decipher the encrypted message by following a number of rules and steps to unlock the code.

## THE COLUMNAR TRANSPOSITION CIPHER

You will need to know some crucial elements of how a columnar transposition works in order to decipher the encrypted message.

1. The encrypted message (the ciphertext) must be laid out into columns and rows of a fixed number. The number of columns is dictated by the number of letters provided in a key (a code word used to unlock the encryption). For example, the key "A N D" would mean a three-column setup.

2. The column length (number of rows) must be calculated.

3. In a transposition cipher, numbers are attributed to the letters within the key word, based on the hierarchy of their placement in the alphabet. For example: the key "A N D" would be attributed the numbers 1, 3, 2, with "A" being the first letter within the word to be found in the alphabet, "N" being the third letter within the word found in the alphabet, and "D" being the second.

4. You must set up the columnar transposition (in columns and rows) before applying the key.

5. In a columnar transposition, the ciphertext is read not in a conventional left-to-right way, but in columns from top to bottom.

You have been provided with the following:
1. The secret message encrypted into a cipher
2. The key
3. A tip for the initial stage of decryption
4. A decryption diagram (showing a four-letter key and twelve-letter ciphertext)

1. Ciphertext:
ANVEIIAIECHEOLUGIVRNYEIRVDMERTUECDBNDYAAOBSEEIELERVDEALMTANE

2. Key: F R I D A Y

3. Column length = number of letters in ciphertext / number of letters in key

4. Ciphertext: ⬤⊙❖❖■⬤■⬤■⊙❖⊙

| Cipher | 1 2 3 4 | Key | 2 1 4 3 |
|--------|---------|-----|---------|
| ➔ | ⬤ ❖ ■ ⊙ | ➔ | ❖ ⬤ ⊙ ■ |
| | ⊙ ■ ⬤ ❖ | | ■ ⊙ ❖ ⬤ |
| | ❖ ⬤ ■ ⊙ | | ⬤ ❖ ⊙ ■ |

USE THIS SPACE FOR YOUR WORKINGS

---

# DIGITAL INTELLIGENCE

Agents must be mindful of the online battlefield and digital espionage. With so much of the world connected, there is a huge focus on the way in which social media and news can be manipulated, directed as propaganda, and used by enemy states. Financial and military systems can be compromised. Electronic files can be manipulated. Secret data can be encrypted and hidden, and moved freely without detection.

This hiding of data within a digital image is known as steganography. The file looks ordinary in every way except for very subtle changes to its setup, making the secrets it hides almost entirely undetectable. The file and its hidden contents can be sent openly without alerting suspicion. The secret data can then be extracted at its destination. Hidden messages can be sent in many ways; in edit tracker on word-processed documents, hidden in a file's source code, or within pixels. Subtle changes in the RGB ratio of single pixels (a combination of the colors red, blue, and green form the color of a pixel) can allow one image to be hidden within another. The image is revealed when the amended pixels are isolated, having been located via the source code.

You have been sent a file containing an image. You know that a secret message is hidden within the RGB values of the nine pixels in the top right-hand corner. Can you decipher the steganographic message? The key is shown below:

A = 1
R = +50          G = +100          B = +150

1. R = 55   G = 118   B = 151

2. R = 69   G = 105   B = 151

3. R = 62   G = 112   B = 168

4. R = 55   G = 103   B = 165

5. R = 68   G = 104   B = 169

6. R = 59   G = 113   B = 163

7. R = 55   G = 104   B = 159

8. R = 51   G = 120   B = 155

9. R = 62   G = 125   B = 150

USE THIS SPACE FOR YOUR WORKINGS

# DISARMING A GUNMAN

Dangerous scenarios can arise at any given time. Seemingly safe situations can escalate into life-threatening moments. A confrontation with an armed assailant is one such scenario. As a secret agent, you must be able to react with speed, calm, and efficiency. Knowledge of how to react to a gun pointed at you is essential. Below are four possible reaction-scenarios in an armed confrontation. Only one is the correct response. Can you determine which one will keep you alive?

1. Make a quick, bold movement toward the gunman, attacking him any which way you can: punch to the ribs, palm into the nose. Be violent and ultra-aggressive.

2. Run away as fast as you can, moving as quickly as possible to a position of safety. Use any barriers between you and the gunman on the way, such as trees and parked cars. Get distance and protection between you and the gunman.

3. Make a short, sharp, decisive grab for the gun, pushing and twisting it so that it no longer points toward you. The twisting action will break the gunman's trigger finger. Keep moving your feet to ensure your weight is over the gun and pointing away from you. Retrieve the gun, step back, and point it at your assailant.

4. Scream, shout, and holler in an attempt to draw attention from others to your situation. This will take confidence away from the gunman. In the midst of the panic, he is likely to flee from the scene, leaving you to run in the opposite direction toward safety.

ANSWER:

# SURVEILLANCE TECHNIQUES

The classic method of human surveillance, with agents monitoring the movements of potential enemies, still remains relevant and important in the modern world of espionage. The digital age has brought with it new factors and techniques of surveillance. There is constant interplay of surveillance and avoidance of detection. Agents must seek to observe the activities of potential foreign enemies while guarding against being observed themselves. Agents must be mindful of every possible way in which security can be breached for intelligence collection, and equally how to guard against foreign agents doing the same. (Televisions, cell phones, and antivirus software are all vulnerable to hacking. Sounds, images, and private text messages can be tapped, even when encrypted.)

Below are five surveillance gadgets and techniques. One of them is not a true gadget or technique. Which one is the intruder?

☐ A. Hidden-camera detection apps
An app can be used to turn a cell phone into a detection tool using magnetic sensors. The user points the phone, scanning objects. Any hidden cameras are flagged via the app.

☐ B. Laser microphones
A laser is beamed through a window, onto an object such as a picture on a wall. The object vibrates when sound waves are present. The laser reflects these vibrations, returning them to a receiver that converts the beam to an audio signal. Sound can be recorded and conversations listened to.

☐ C. Ring cameras
Micro cameras so small they are hidden in rings and worn as jewelry.

☐ D. Night vision pills
Pills can be taken that coat the retina with graphene, a substance that enables the full infrared spectrum and ultraviolet light to penetrate the eye, producing sensitive night vision.

☐ E. Use of a safe house
A location where agents can undertake clandestine observations.

# PRISONER: TRICKS AND COUNTER TRICKS

You may find yourself on either side of the dividing line when it comes to a hostage situation or prisoner interrogation. You need to know techniques and tricks of the trade to coax intelligence from detainees. You also need to know how to avoid releasing valuable information, if you are taken prisoner yourself. Below are a series of tricks, the aim of the trick, and possible counters to both look out for and to pursue depending upon which side of the interrogation table you are sitting. In each case, one of the counters is the option you should take. Can you spot which one?

1. Trick: Ask the prisoner why they think they have been arrested.
Aim: Sometimes the detainee will make unexpected disclosures.
Counter:
☐ A. Say you have no idea. Or a basic statement referring to your cover story
☐ B. Tell the interrogator what you believe they want you to say

2. Trick: Accuse them of fabricated activities.
Aim: In giving an alibi, the detainee may disclose where they actually were at the given time.
Counter:
☐ A. Simply deny
☐ B. Ensure any alibi is foolproof

3. Trick: Have the detainee fill out forms.
Aim: To have evidence of their handwriting style.
Counter:
☐ A. Always write anything in distorted writing
☐ B. Always refuse

4. Trick: Put them in a room with other "prisoners" and encourage them to engage in conversation.
Aim: For small clues to their activities to surface.
Counter:
☐ A. Simply do not speak to anybody.
☐ B. Make it a rule to never engage in seemingly harmless conversations.

5. Trick: Ask the detainee to run through their cover story backward.
Aim: Inconsistencies may become apparent, which can be used to break their cover story.
Counter:
☐ A. Refuse on the grounds that it is nonsensical.
☐ B. Learn your cover story backward and memorize it.

6. Trick: Stare in silence at the bridge of the detainee's nose.
Aim: To look through the person, which is highly unsettling. Coupled with a sustained silence, the detainee may feel compelled to speak.
Counter:
☐ A. Stare back.
☐ B. Close your eyes.

7. Trick: Talk nonsense to the detainee, asking questions that make no sense.
Aim: To make them think they are losing their mind.
Counter:
☐ A. Keep the interrogator asking nonsensical questions in order to gain more time.
☐ B. Talk nonsense back to them.

8. Trick: Using a dummy tape recorder, which is "turned off" and the detainee told the conversation is completely private. Whereas in fact the whole conversation is being recorded by a hidden recording device.
Aim: For the detainee to reveal information.
Counter:
☐ A. Understand no interrogation is ever "completely private."
☐ B. Aim to show trust has been developed by offering one or two pieces of nonvital information.

# MORSE CODE MESSAGE

Morse code has been used as a method to send coded messages and universal signals since the 1830s. It was developed as a character-encoding technique used in telecommunications. Each letter of the alphabet has a unique code based on varying lengths of electrical impulses sent over telephone wires to a receiver. The coded pulses of "dots" and "dashes" can also be used to encode written messages as well as audio messages sent as "dits" and "dahs." Morse code is still used by international agencies across the world, including the CIA. As an agent, knowledge of Morse code is needed.

The encoding chart below shows the dots and dashes assigned to numbers and letters of the alphabet. The letters most commonly used are assigned shorter codes (e.g., "E" and "T").

| | | | | | | | |
|---|---|---|---|---|---|---|---|
| A | •— | J | •——— | S | ••• | 1 | •———— |
| B | —••• | K | —•— | T | — | 2 | ••——— |
| C | —•—• | L | •—•• | U | ••— | 3 | •••—— |
| D | —•• | M | —— | V | •••— | 4 | ••••— |
| E | • | N | —• | W | •—— | 5 | ••••• |
| F | ••—• | O | ——— | X | —••— | 6 | —•••• |
| G | ——• | P | •——• | Y | —•—— | 7 | ——••• |
| H | •••• | Q | ——•— | Z | ——•• | 8 | ———•• |
| I | •• | R | •—• | | | 9 | ————• |
| | | | | | | 0 | ————— |

Using the encoding chart (or having memorized the encoding system!), can you decipher the message in Morse code below?

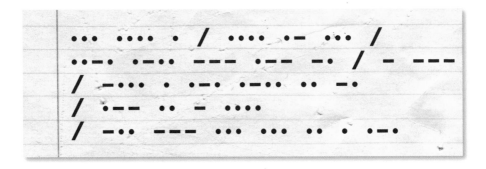

Did you spot the Morse code message on the front cover? What does it say?

# ANSWERS

# LOGIC AND LATERAL THINKING

**CRACK THE SAFE** (pages 10–11)
17, 34, 40 (These are the only three numbers that cannot be calculated by adding together two numbers from within the inner circle.)

**NEXT ASSIGNMENT** (pages 12–13)
The end of World War II: 1945
September 11 attack on the United States: 2001
The end of the U.S. Civil War: 1865
The Berlin Wall comes down: 1989
Start of covert operation: 6/18/2019

**WHAT DID SHE DO?** (page 14)
(D) She stopped the car, opened the hood, and said, "Thank goodness you've come along—I think I have a problem with my carburetor."

**HIDDEN IN NUMBERS** (page 15)
Johannes is Agent 34
J = 4, O = 6, H = 3, A = 1, N = 5, E = 2, S = 8
Agent 12's message: BILL SEES. LEE IS ILL. SHE SELLS SHOES (turn the book 180 degrees to read the numbers as letters).

**SWITCHED DRINKS?** (page 16)
Tilt the glass (see diagram below). If the liquid reaches points A and C without spilling, then the glass is not more than half full.

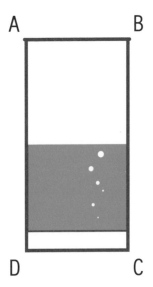

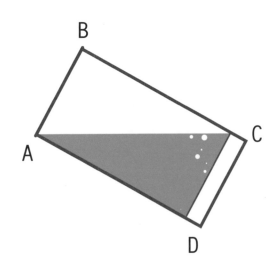

## STEPS TO FREEDOM
(page 17)

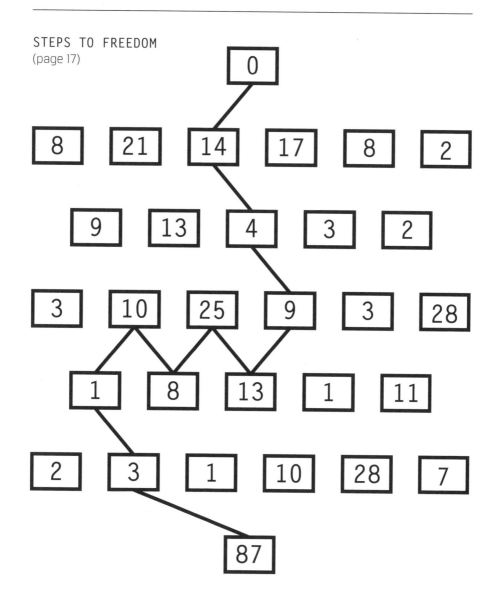

## TWO TRAINS (page 18)
They will meet at station 10 at 7:00 p.m.

# ANSWERS

## THE SAFEST ROUTE (page 19)

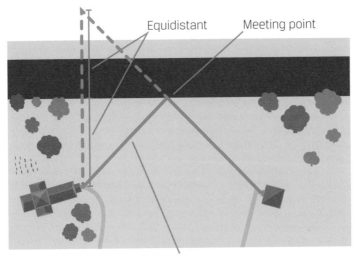

Equidistant    Meeting point

Quickest route

## NINE DOTS (page 20)

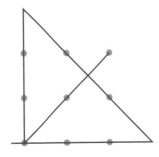

## RETRIEVING THE DOCUMENTS (page 21)

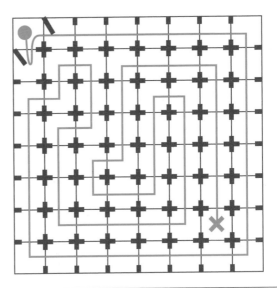

**MENTAL AGILITY** (pages 22–24)

1. The double agent has escaped to Algiers with file.
2. 204
3. The steel structure expands in the heat of the sun and so is 6 inches higher in the summer, making it higher to climb.
4. Noon (Dr. Awkward is a palindrome—they read the same backward—and his favorite time of the day is palindromic)
5. The human brain (its home is the body)
6. 66 (multiply the sum shown + multiply the first number of the sum by itself: [6 x 5 = 30] + [6 x 6 = 3] = 66)
7. They are all palindromic years
- 1661—The first banknotes in Europe are issued by Sweden.
- 1771—Thomas Cook returns to the Western World from his around-the-world voyage, during which he discovered Australia.
- 1881—U.S. president James A. Garfield is assassinated.
- 1991—The USSR is dissolved, bringing about the end of the Cold War.
8. 110 (multiply the number by the number next in sequence: 2 x 3 = 6, 3 x 4 = 12 . . . 10 x 11 = 110)
9. China (the traditional gift for a 20th wedding anniversary is china)
10. See table at the bottom of the page

**DRINKING LIMITS** (page 25)

Fill glass A, so you have 700ml. Pour into glass B, leaving 200ml in A and 500ml in B. Empty B into the empty third glass. Pour A into B, so A has 0ml and B has 200ml. Fill A, so that it has 700ml, and empty it into B until B is full. B now has 500ml, leaving A with 400ml.

**THE FINAL MEETING** (page 26)

Saturday 8:30 a.m. The hour is derived from the number of letters in the day of the meeting (Saturday = 8). The minutes are derived from the number of letters in the previous day's meeting, broken down into 5-minute segments (Friday: 6 x 5 minutes = 30 minutes).

**THE MILLIONAIRE** (page 27)

27 days

*Group connection*

| | | | | |
|---|---|---|---|---|
| Cue | Rack | Stripes | Pocket | Billiard terms |
| Ball | Sabbath | Jack | Bird | Black |
| Nails | Foil | Golf club | Pot | Things made of aluminum |
| Berlin | Great | Wailing | Peace | Famous walls |

# ANSWERS

## MATCHSTICKS (pages 28–31)

1.

2.

3.

4.

5.

6.

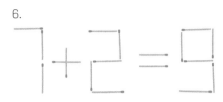

10.

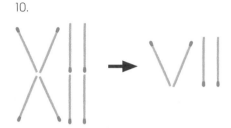

7.

8. 81151: Move two matchsticks from the zero and place them at the front of the number to make 15118. Then rotate the page to make 81151.

A TIMELY MEETING (page 32)
1:05 p.m. and 27 seconds. When the minute and hour hands next meet will perhaps logically be 1:05 p.m. However, no sooner has the minute hand reached 1:05 p.m. than the hour hand has already started to move onward toward 2:00 p.m. Therefore, it must be some time after 1:05 p.m. When the hour hand is at 1:00 p.m., it will take 11 hours to reach parity at noon again. Therefore, the minute hand has to travel 60 minutes 11 times (11 revolutions) for the two hands to reach this parity. If we break this down into how many minutes the hour hand travels in one revolution of the minute hand, we must calculate 60/11 = 5 minutes, 27 seconds. Therefore, the meeting will start at exactly 1:05 p.m. and 27 seconds.

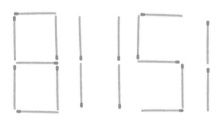

9.

# ANSWERS

## A CRIME SCENE (page 33)

The clue: the man appears to have been using the central urinal. The explanation: in the event all three urinals are available, it is unusual for a man to choose to use the central urinal. If another user comes in, they would be forced to stand next to each other. If there is one man already using the urinal, they are therefore likely to be using the first or third urinal. In this scenario the murdered man is likely to have chosen to stand at the urinal farthest away. Only if the first and third urinals were in use by two other men would the man have chosen to use the central urinal.

## THE SHOPPING LIST (page 34)

Pi rounded down = 3.14
Two dates:
Christmas Day = 12/25
Valentine's Day = 2/14
3141225214
Add these digits to get 25
Get off at the 25th floor

## FOUR HATS (page 35)

The answer is C. He is certain because he knows that if D could see two white hats he would speak out immediately. His silence means that he cannot see two white hats. Therefore, C knows he must be wearing a black hat.

## ELEVEN GRENADES (page 36)

If you keep the defective grenade in the initial count you can divide half of them = 6, divide into a quarter = 3, divide a sixth = 2. Then you take out the defective grenade and are left with the eleven grenades while maintaining the instructions.

## HOW MANY HANDSHAKES? (page 37)

6

## THE BRIEFCASE (page 38)

The combination is 1876
The seven possible solutions are:
938 + 938 = 1876
928 + 928 = 1856
867 + 867 = 1734
846 + 846 = 1692
836 + 836 = 1672
765 + 765 = 1530
734 + 734 = 1468

## NUMBER SQUARES (page 39)

* = 1
All the numbers in each square added together make 20, so * has to be 1.

## SIX PENCILS (page 40)

Form a three-dimensional tetrahedron (three pencils to form the base; three pencils projecting from the base and meeting in a point to form the three equilateral sides)

## LINKING THE PORTS (page 41)

## SECRETS ON A BOOKSHELF
(page 42)
*Madam Secretary* by Madeleine Albright and *The Deified Self* by James McFarlane. They both contain palindromes within their titles.

## HIDDEN CARGO (page 43)
002: 10:20 a.m.
003: 3:40 p.m.

## CODE NAME RIDDLES
(pages 44–45)
1. Age
2. Postage stamp
3. 1963 is the number of the hospital room in which she was born
4. Silence
5. Eating watermelon
6. Anchor
7. Shadow
8. Envelope
9. Nothing—the time of the meeting is 11:00 p.m. (The word "envelope" contains the word "eleven," and the word "nothing" contains the word "night." Eleven at night = 11:00 p.m.)

# INTERNATIONAL AFFAIRS

**GLOBAL LINKS** (pages 48–49)
1. Los Angeles (they are all the biggest ports of their respective countries).
2. Any one of Bangladesh, Japan, Namibia, or Rwanda (they all have suns represented on their flag).
3. Trees (Canada has a maple leaf, Lebanon a cedar tree, and Equatorial Guinea a silk cotton tree).
4. They are the only two countries with a map of the country on their flag.
5. They both have birds represented on them.
6. Sao Paulo (they are all the most populated cities in their respective countries).
7. The Bering Strait (in winter an ice field is formed, linking the two countries, and the continents of Asia and North America).
8. A = Russia, B = Algeria, C = Brazil, D = Canada, E = 2. France. The countries shown are the biggest nations in their respective continents. Russia (Asia), Algeria (Africa), Brazil (South America), Canada (North America), France (Europe).

**FLAGS OF THE WORLD**
(pages 50–51)
1. A = Romania, B = Mongolia, C = Saudi Arabia, D = Argentina
2.1 Nepal
2.2 It is the only non-quadrilateral national flag.
3.1 27

3.2 (Australia, Burundi, Denmark, Dominica, Dominican Republic, Fiji, Finland, Georgia, Greece, Iceland, Jamaica, Marshall Islands, Malta, Moldova, Montenegro, New Zealand, Norway, Portugal, San Marino, Serbia, Slovakia, Spain, Sweden, Switzerland, Tonga, Tuvalu, United Kingdom)
4. B

**CONFLICT ZONE FACT FILES**
(pages 52–55)
1. Israel, 2. Nigeria, 3. North Korea, 4. Myanmar

**WORLD INTELLIGENCE AGENCIES**
(pages 56–57)
1. (G), 2. (C), 3. (K), 4. (D), 5. (L), 6. (A), 7. (B), 8. (F), 9. (I), 10. (J), 11. (N), 12. (M), 13. (E), 14. (O), 15. (H)

**WHERE ARE YOU?
MOUNTAIN RANGES** (page 58)
1. (C) Drakensberg
2. (B) Andes
3. (A) Alps
4. (D) Himalayas

**A NUMBERS GAME** (page 59)
1. 1.4 billion
2. 29,029
3. 41,820
4. 810,815
5. 3212
6. 36.1 million
7. 1.1 billion
8. 83.94 billion

## WHAT COMES NEXT? (pages 60–61)
1. Dulles (they are all airports)
2. Parliament (they are all names of each nation's parliament)
3. Nikkei (they are all stock market indexes)
4. Any Irish militant separatist/ liberation group (e.g., IRA, Orange Volunteers, Red Hand Defenders)
5. Nelson Mandela and F. W. de Clerk, South Africa (they are all Nobel Peace Prize winners)
6. Euro (they are all currencies)
7. Bikini Atoll (they are all nuclear testing sites)
8. Christ the Redeemer (they are all the most visited tourist attraction in their respective country)
9. Mount Ararat (they are all the highest mountain in their respective country)
10. Portuguese (they are all official state languages)

## ABANDONED LOCATIONS
(pages 62–63)
1. Pripyat, Chernobyl (Ukraine)
2. Six Flags, New Orleans (United States)
3. Saddam Hussein's palace (Iraq)
4. Kolmanskop (Namibia)
5. Humderstone and Santa Laura, Atacama Desert (Chile)

## GLOBAL GEOGRAPHY QUIZ
(pages 64–67)
1. 1. Pacific, 2. Atlantic, 3. Indian, 4. Southern, 5. Arctic
2. The Atlantic and Pacific Oceans are so large they are often divided at the equator, with the north and south classed as divided entities. This gives us North and South Atlantic and North and South Pacific, giving us the "Seven Seas."
3. 97.5%
4. The melting of all the world's surface ice. Of the 2.5% of the world's fresh water, two-thirds is locked into the ice sheets of the Antarctic and the world's mountain glaciers. If they were to melt, the water would be unlocked, causing a catastrophic rise in sea levels.
5. It is showing the largest 25 countries in descending order of size.
6. Azerbaijan, Georgia, Kazakhstan, Russia, and Turkey
7. Armenia and Cyprus
8. Andes (7,000km; 4,350 miles) Venezuela, Colombia, Ecuador, Peru, Bolivia, Chile, Argentina
9. The world's land boundaries
10. Iguazú Falls, Argentina
11: The Suez Canal
12: It is the world's greatest earthquake and volcano zone, extending from Chile to New Zealand.

# ANSWERS

## SCRAMBLED CAPITAL CITIES
(page 68)
1. CARACAS
2. BOGOTÁ
3. BUENOS AIRES
4. SANTIAGO
5. SARAJEVO
6. HAVANA
7. JAKARTA
8. ISLAMABAD
9. BERLIN
10. PARIS
11. WARSAW
12. STOCKHOLM
13. KUALA LUMPUR
14. MOSCOW
15. SEOUL
16. CAIRO
17. CANBERRA
18. NAIROBI

## WHERE ARE YOU? RIVERS
(page 69)
1. Thames, London (UK)
2. Amazon (Bolivia, Brazil, Colombia, Ecuador, Peru, Venezuela)
3. Nile (Tanzania, Uganda, Rwanda, Burundi, the Democratic Republic of the Congo, Kenya, Ethiopia, Eritrea, South Sudan, Sudan, and Egypt)
4. Mississippi (United States)

## STARS (pages 70-71)
1. Morocco
2. United States
3. Pakistan
4. Panama
5. North Korea
6. Bosnia and Herzegovina
7. China
8. Venezuela
9. Philippines
10. Australia
11. Brazil
12. Israel

## COCKTAIL MENU (pages 72-73)
1. Argentina
2. Barbados
3. El Salvador
4. Liberia
5. Spain
6. Malta
7. Lichtenstein
8. Belarus
9. India
10. Nauru

## HUMAN GEOGRAPHY QUIZ
(pages 74-75)
1. (Figures 2017, est. in millions) China 1,379; India 1,282; United States 327; Indonesia 261; Brazil 207; Pakistan 205; Nigeria 191; Bangladesh 158; Russia 142; Japan 126
2. China and India
3. They represent the extremes of population density. Macau is the world's most densely populated country and Greenland the least.
4. Mandarin Chinese (12%), Spanish (6%), English (5%), Arabic (5%)
5. 150
6. Christianity 31%, Islam 23%, Hinduism 15%, Buddhism 7%
7. $17,500
8. 82%

## HUMAN DISPLACEMENT
(pages 76–77)
1. Jordan
2. Turkey
3. Pakistan
4. Lebanon
5. Iran
6. Ethiopia
7. Kenya
8. Uganda
9. Democratic Republic of Congo
10. Chad

## GEO-ECONOMICS AND CRUDE OIL
(pages 78–79)
1. Venezuela, Saudi Arabia, and Canada
2. Venezuela
3. Nigeria
4. Iraq, Iran, Russia, Saudi Arabia, United States
5. United States
6. Canada
7. Iran
8. (B) Geopolitics

## GEO-ECONOMIC DEPENDENCIES: UNITED STATES (page 80)
1. West Bank/Gaza ($370)
2. Israel ($367)
3. Jordan ($188)
4. Afghanistan ($148)
5. Lebanon ($84)

## GEO-ECONOMIC DEPENDENCIES: CHINA (page 81)
1. Australia (34%)
2. Taiwan (26%)
3. Korea (25%)
4. Chile (23%)
5.= Japan (19%)
5.= Peru (19%)
7. Brazil (18%)
8=. Malaysia (12%)
8.= Thailand (12%)
10. Indonesia (10%)

## THE ONLINE BATTLEFIELD
(pages 82–83)
United States = 82% (18 segments) shaded, equating to 265 million online/59 million off-line
China = 51% (47 segments) shaded, equating to 702 million online/677 million off-line
Source: Statista Digital Market Outlook, 2016

## TERRORIST GROUPS (pages 84–85)
1. Hezbollah
2. Al-Qaeda in Iraq
3. Al-Qaeda in the Islamic Maghreb
4. Harkat-ul-Mujahideen
5. Ansaru
6. Jamiat-e Islami
7. Islamic Jihad Movement in Palestine
8. New People's Army of the Philippines
9. Jaish-e-Mohammed
10. Eastern Indonesian Mujahideen
11. Lashkar-e-Jhangvi
12. Turkistan Islamic Party

# MEMORY AND PERCEPTION

## MENTAL SELF-ROTATION (pages 88–91)
1. 2 left turns, 1 right turn
2. 3 left turns, 3 right turns
3. 5 left turns, 5 right turns
4. 6 left turns, 8 right turns

## SPOT THE DIFFERENCES (pages 92–93)

## SOMETHING ODD (pages 94–95)

1. This is typically a pangram, meaning it includes all the letters in the alphabet (in this case the word "jumps" has been replaced with "jumped" and so is missing the letter "s").
2. Has no letter "e."
3. Only has the vowel "e" and is missing every other vowel.
4. Every letter "h" is in italic.
5. It is odd that the identity of the fourth child is being asked, considering all four children have already been mentioned.

## FINDING THE ERROR (page 96)

Did you spot the repeated "the" in the opening paragraph?

## HOW MANY HOLES? (page 97)

There are eight holes—at the neck, base, and end of the arms. There are also two holes at the front and two at the back (since you can see the background through these holes).

# ANSWERS

## MORNING, NOON, OR NIGHT
(pages 98–99)
1. 7:00 p.m.
If you look at the picture with the UK Parliament on the left and Portculis House on the right, and then look at Big Ben on a map, you can work out that the photo is facing west, so it must be a sunset, and hence 7:00 p.m.
2. 12:00 p.m.
There are a number of clues. The sun is out, yet the Flatiron building (in New York) is casting no shadow, has no shadow on either of its sides, and is casting no shadow on the building behind. The shadows cast by the people and car are directly underneath, showing that it is the peak of the midday sun.

3. 6:30 p.m.
Christ the Redeemer faces the rising sun and the people of Rio de Janeiro to the east. The sun is behind it, so it is therefore sunset.
4. 7:00 a.m.
In New York, even-numbered streets typically run toward the east, with odd-numbered streets typically running toward the west. The sign shows West 33rd Street, and the sun is behind this west-facing street sign. The sun is rising from the east, and therefore it is the morning.

## RANDOM ICONS (pages 100–101)
1. A pair of circles
2. A white star in a red circle
3. A pentagon

## AIRDROP (page 102)

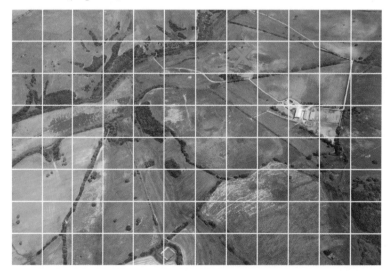

## PRISON BREAK (page 103)

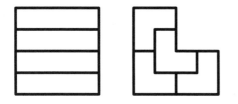

## ENEMY LOCATION (pages 108–109)

1.

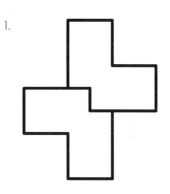

## SURVEILLANCE RISK (pages 104–105)
Green is the safest route.

| Route | Distance | Risk factor | Exposure risk |
|-------|----------|-------------|---------------|
| Blue | 3.7 miles | 2.5 | 9.25 |
| Red | 3.5 miles | 3 | 10.5 |
| Green | 4 miles | 2.25 | 9 |
| Yellow | 4.6 miles | 2 | 9.2 |

2.

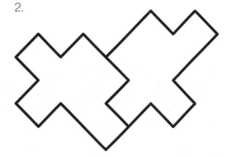

## FLAG CONNECTIONS (page 106)
Answer: Montenegro is the only flag that contains an animal that is not a bird. The bird is also the only fictional bird—a two-headed eagle.

## THE MIRROR TEST (page 107)
1. The minimum possible height of the mirror is half your height. And it should be positioned with the top of the mirror in line with a point that is halfway between your eyes and the top of your head.
2. (C) You see the same amount of your body. You get smaller as you step backward, but the same amount of your body is obscured.

3.

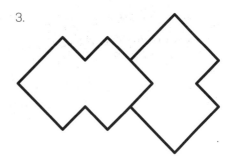

# ANSWERS

## RANDOM OBJECTS MEMORY TEST
(pages 110–113)
1. Pencil, key, book
2. (B) Paintbrush
3. Scissors
4. Pencil
5. Key, envelope
6. (C) Flag
7. Airplane, pencil, floppy disk, key, gun, bomb, book, knife, scissors, bell
8. Star, skull and crossbones, pen, envelope, flower, snowflake, telephone, candle, egg timer, glasses
9. 8745

## MEMORIZING NUMBERS: VEHICLE REGISTRATION PLATES
(pages 114–116)
1. CH 182 747
2. C 14 837 27
3. ZW 27 843 D
4. GB 746 912
5. DK 9988 76
6. PK 64 7 29A

## SPOT THE DIFFERENCES (pages 118–121)

# ANSWERS

## X-RAY OBSERVATION

(pages 122–123)
The small aerosol can has
been removed.

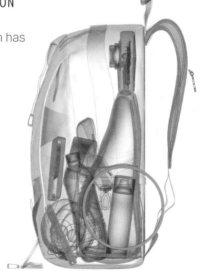

## QUICK PERCEPTION TESTS
(pages 124–125)
1. (E)
2. Neither, they are both the same size
3. Three

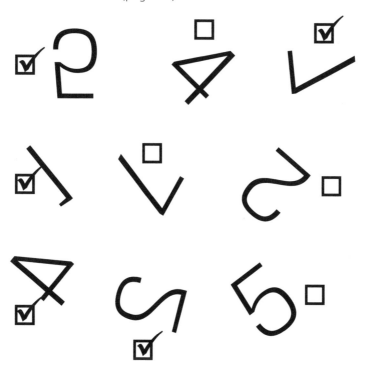

4. The circle in a square. It takes up 78% of the area; the square in a circle takes up 64%

5. It is a representation of the brain, rotated 180 degrees

## SAY WHAT YOU SEE (page 126)
Square, star, circle, triangle, star
Circle, star, circle, square, circle
Triangle, square, star, square, triangle

## MIRRORED NUMBERS (page 127)

# WORLD HISTORY AND CONFLICT

## WHAT IS BEING SHOWN HERE?
(pages 130–133)
1. The reach of Soviet nuclear missiles from the Bay of Pigs (1962)
2. John F. Kennedy's "Ich Bin ein Berliner" speech (1963)
3. The White House/Kremlin hotline set up following the Cuban Missile Crisis (1963)
4. During John F. Kennedy's presidency the White House was known as Camelot, due to the perceived drama of the Kennedy family.
5. The first McDonald's restaurant opens in Pushkin Square, Moscow, symbolizing the end of the Cold War.
6. Representing the nonviolent revolutions of 1989 in Poland, Hungary, East Germany, Czechoslovakia, and Bulgaria

## WEAPONS OF WAR (page 134)
1. World War I (France used tear gas, or ethyl bromoacetate)
2. The Manhattan Project
3. UK and Canada
4. Hiroshima and Nagasaki
5. Agent Orange
6. Sarin

## TECH (page 135)
1. Colossus
2. Enigma
3. 1961
4. Develop a system to neutralize nuclear weapons
5. Star Wars
6. Telstar 1

## WORLD LEADERS AT THE OUTBREAK OF WAR
(pages 136–137)
WORLD WAR I (1914)
Germany: Kaiser Wilhelm II
Russia: Czar Nicholas II
UK: David Lloyd George
United States: Woodrow Wilson

WORLD WAR II (1939)
Germany: Adolf Hitler
Russia: Joseph Stalin
UK: Neville Chamberlain
United States: Franklin D. Roosevelt

2ND IRAQ WAR (2003)
Germany: Gerhard Schröder
Russia: Vladimir Putin
UK: Tony Blair
United States: George W. Bush

## WITNESSES OF HISTORY
(pages 138–140)
1. The assassination of U.S. president William McKinley in 1901
2. The liberation of Paris from the Nazis
3. The construction of the Berlin Wall
4. Vietnam
5. The Vietnam War, 1955–75
6. The assassination of Dr. Martin Luther King Jr. in 1968
7. An unknown Chinese protester standing in front of a tank during the Tiananmen Square Massacre in 1989
8. He claims actually to have said, "One small step for a man…"

## HISTORY IN NUMBERS (page 141)
1. 4
2. 100
3. 17
4. 13
5. 15 billion billion

## MAP OF CHANGE (pages 142–143)
1. Independence from colonial rule
2. The year each country gained its independence
3. The colonial power from which each country gained its independence
4. Liberia and Ethiopia
5. They are the only two African countries that were not colonized in the nineteenth-century "Scramble for Africa."

## FAMOUS FIRSTS (page 144)
1. 1839
2. 1911
3. 1967
4. 1893
5. 1973
6. 1903
7. 1963
8. 1868

## SPANNING THE GLOBE (page 145)
1. Egypt
2. Egypt
3. Mexico
4. Indonesia
5. Mexico
6. Indonesia

## MIXED-UP QUOTES (page 146)
1. "Whoever is happy will make others happy too." —Anne Frank

2. "The greatest glory in living lies not in never falling, but in rising every time we fall." —Nelson Mandela

3. "When you reach the end of your rope, tie a knot in it and hang on." —Franklin D. Roosevelt

4. "I have learned over the years that when one's mind is made up, this diminishes fear." —Rosa Parks

# ANSWERS

## HISTORICAL LINKS (page 147)
They all occurred on the same day:
October 29

## A TO Z QUIZ (pages 148–151)
1. ANZAC
2. Berners-Lee
3. Czechoslovakia
4. Denmark
5. Eisenhower (Dwight)
6. Franco
7. Glasnost
8. Hirohito
9. Intifada
10. Jakarta
11. Knives
12. Los Angeles
13. Maastricht
14. Nixon (Richard)
15. Oppenheimer (J. Robert)
16. Perestroika
17. Quebec
18. Robben
19. Sri Lanka
20. Tet Offensive
21. Urals
22. Venezuela
23. Waco
24. X-ray
25. Year
26. Zog (King Zog I)

## ODD ONE OUT (page 152)
Rawhide. It was Ronald Reagan's
personal code name.

## PICTURE QUIZ (page 153)
1. Henry Kissinger
2. Malcolm X
3. Margaret Thatcher
4. Indira Gandhi
5. Colin Powell
6. Leonid Brezhnev
7. Robert Mugabe
8. Madeleine Albright
9. Manuel Noriega

## FIND THE LINK (page 154)
1. George Washington, 1776 (they were
all their respective country's first
leader)
2. Any battle with something relating
to water in its name (e.g., Attack on
Pearl Harbor, 1941)
3. Any country winning a war of
independence (e.g., Bangladesh
Liberation War [from Pakistan], 1971)

## UNSCRAMBLE (page 155)
1. ROMMEL
2. SCHWARZKOPF
3. EISENHOWER
4. MACARTHUR
5. FRANCO
6. GUEVARA
7. RICHARD FEYNMAN
8. ALBERT EINSTEIN
9. MARIE CURIE
10. SIGMUND FREUD
11. IVAN PAVLOV
12. ROSALIND FRANKLIN

## COLD WAR TIMELINE
(pages 156–157)
1. Conference
2. Czechoslovakia
3. Airlift
4. Korean
5. Warsaw
6. Dog
7. Pigs
8. Charlie
9. Cuban
10. Spring
11. Paris
12. Moscow
13 Velvet

## HISTORICAL SPEECHES (page 158)
1. "I have a dream"
—Martin Luther King (1963)
2. "Ich bin ein Berliner"
—John F. Kennedy (1963)
3. "I am prepared to die"
—Nelson Mandela (1964)
4. "The wind of change"
—Harold MacMillan (1960)
5. "We will never surrender"
—Winston Churchill (1940)
6. "The only thing we have to fear is fear itself"
—Franklin D. Roosevelt (1933)

## FIND THE MISSING NUMBERS
(page 159)
1. 9
2. 9
3. 3
4. 1
5. 7
6. 13

## DICTATORS AND DESPOTS
(pages 160–161)
1. D
2. A
3. F
4. E
5. C
6. B

# TECHNIQUES

**INVISIBLE INK** (pages 164–165)
Business card hidden message:
"Ask the bell boy for the papers"
(deciphered using the hotel's address
as an anagram, but ignoring the
words/letters as indicated by Rignore
– England, UK)

Hotel headed notepaper message:
"Reach advance post. Reroute ship.
Refuse free help" (deciphered using
the hotel's address as an anagram)

**COINS AND BANKNOTES** (pages 166–168)

1.

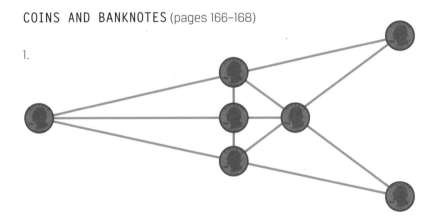

2.

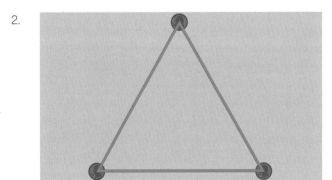

3.

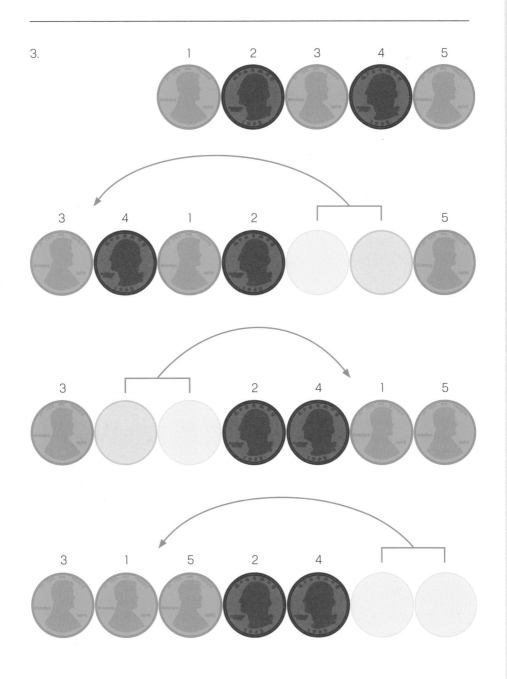

# ANSWERS

## 638 TECHNIQUES TO KILL CASTRO (page 169)
2 (Castro's wife was loyal to him)
5 (Castro was a lover of chess, but his games passed without incident)

## THE INTERROGATION ROOM (pages 170–171)
1. The tape recorder/one interrogator. An interrogator interviewing a detainee should not control a tape recorder.
2. Notepad and pen (see above)
3. The lamp. The light source should be directed from behind the interrogator to obscure their face and to unsettle the detainee.
4. The clock. The walls should be bare to avoid any feeling of comfort and familiarity with the environment.
5. The light switch. There should be no sense of even the slightest bit of control.
6. The door. The door should not be next to the detainee. Ideally it would be at the end of a relatively long corridor so that the detainee has an uncomfortable walk toward the intimidating interrogator.

## MEALTIME? (pages 172–173)
The interrogators are playing with the detainee's body clock and sense of time by speeding up and slowing down the clock on the cell wall. And they are mirroring the three meals of the day to this distorted view of time.

## "WHAT IF" SCENARIOS (page 178)
1. D
2. C—you must be able to move freely with rubble and debris underfoot
3. D

## DEFUSING A BOMB (page 179)
The pink wire

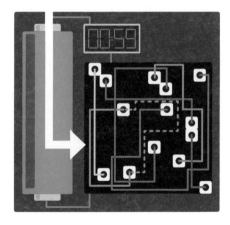

## COMPLEX CIPHERS (pages 180–181)

Step-by-step answer:

ANVEIIAIECHEOLUGIVRNYEIRVDMERTUECDBNDYAAOBSEEIELERVDEALMTANE
Column length = 60 / 6
Column length = 10
ANVEIIAIEC HEOLUGIVRN YEIRVDMERT UECDBNDYAA OBSEEIELER VDEALMTANE
Place ten-letter segmented ciphertext into consecutively numbered columns

```
1 2 3 4 5 6
A H Y U O V
N E E E B D
V O I C S E
E L R D E A
I U V B E L
I G D N I M
A I M D E T
I V E Y L A
E R R A E N
C N T A R E
```

Reorder columns based on the number attribution of the key word FRIDAY

```
F R I D A Y
3 5 4 2 1 6
Y O U H A V
E B E E N D
I S C O V E
R E D L E A
V E B U I L
D I N G I M
M E D I A T
E L Y V I A
R E A R E N
T R A N C E
```

Deciphered text: You have been discovered. Leave building immediately via rear entrance.

# ANSWERS

## DIGITAL INTELLIGENCE
(pages 182–183)
5 18 1   19 5 1   12 12 18   5 3 15   18 4 19
9 13 13   5 4 9   1 20 5   12 25 0
ERA  SEA  LLR  ECO  RDS  IMM  EDI  ATE
LY_
ERASE ALL RECORDS IMMEDIATELY

## DISARMING A GUNMAN
(pages 184–185)
3—Make a short, sharp, decisive grab for the gun, pushing and twisting it, so that it no longer points toward you. The twisting action will break the gunman's trigger finger. Keep moving your feet to ensure your weight is over the gun and pointing away from you. Retrieve the gun, step back, and point it at your assailant. (There is a high chance that the other three options would result in you being shot.)

## SURVEILLANCE TECHNIQUES
(pages 186–187)
D—Graphene night vision contact lenses have been developed, but not graphene pills.

## PRISONER: TRICKS AND COUNTER TRICKS (pages 188–189)
1. B
2. A
3. A
4. B
5. B
6. A
7. A
8. A

## MORSE CODE MESSAGE
(pages 190–191)
SHE HAS FLOWN TO BERLIN WITH DOSSIER

Morse code message on the book cover near the spine:
YOU KNOW MORSE CODE THEN

This book would not have been possible without Matt Windsor, who did such a fantastic job with the design and worked tirelessly to bring the puzzles to life. Big thanks also go to the project editors, Richard Webb and Judith Chamberlain. I would like to thank my mother, Nicki Gillard, who was often asked to solve puzzles and answer questions throughout the process of compiling the book. I would also like to thank Rob Brandt for his excellent illustrations, and puzzle expert Gareth Moore, who put the first draft of the book through its paces.

# PICTURE CREDITS

Images used in this book that are not listed below are in the public domain.

14 © SIA KAMBOU / AFP / Getty Images
26 © chainarong06 | Shutterstock
32 © Jose Gil | Shutterstock
36 © Vakabungo | Shutterstock
37 ©ESB Professional | Shutterstock
38 © Mauro 1969 | Shutterstock
58 top right © Yarr65 | Shutterstock
58 bottom left © Vladislav Gurfinkel | Shutterstock
58 bottom right © Simon Wendler | Shutterstock
62 top © Kamilalala | Shutterstock
62 bottom © KEG-KEG|Shutterstock.com
63 top © Al Orfali | Shutterstock
63 middle © Hang Dinh | Shutterstock
63 bottom © Marisa Estivill | Shutterstock
65 © Anton Shahrai | Shutterstock
67 © Yarr65 | Shutterstock
69 top left © TommoT | Shutterstock
92 © solepsizm | Shutterstock
93 © solepsizm | Shutterstock
97 © Ruslan Kudrin | Shutterstock
98 left © Samot | Shutterstock
98 right © Depositphotos
99 top ©Ksenia Ragosina | Shutterstock
99 bottom © View Apart | Shutterstock
102 © Gabriele Maltinti | Shutterstock
105 © Bardocz Peter | Shutterstock
118 © Cerri Breeze | Shutterstock
119 © Digo Arpi | Shutterstock
120 © Paul Vinten | Shutterstock

121 © Art Konovalov | Shutterstock
122 © David Kasza | Shutterstock
123 © David Kasza | Shutterstock
125 © solarseven | Shutterstock
136 top © Gilles BASSIGNAC
136 bottom © Keystone
137 top left © Getty Images
137 top middle © Creative Commons
137 top right © Getty Images
137 center left © Wojtek Laski
137 bottom right © Hulton Archive
141 © Sean Gallup
142–143 World with Countries - Single Color by FreeVectorMaps.com
147 top left © Getty Images
147 top right © Hulton Archive
147 bottom left © Imagno
147 bottom right © Getty Images
153 top right © Creative Commons
153 center left © Bachrach
153 center right © Francis Apesteguy
153 bottom left © DESMOND KWANDE
153 bottom right © Bettmann
157 © Creative Commons | fotogoocom
160 top left © Bettmann
160 top right © Marcelo Montecino
160 bottom right © Creative Commons | Archives New Zealand
169 © dean bertoncelj | Shutterstock
184 © Kryuchka Yaroslav | Shutterstock

Every effort has been made to credit the copyright holders of the images used in this book. We apologize for any unintentional omissions or errors and will insert the appropriate acknowledgment to any companies or individuals in subsequent editions of the work.